# What No One Ever Tells You About

# STARTING YOUR OWN BUSINESS

## Real Life Start-Up Advice from 101 Successful Entrepreneurs

# Jan Norman

Upstart
Publishing Company®
*Specializing in Small Business Publishing*
a division of Dearborn Publishing Group, Inc.

Acquisitions Editor: Danielle Egan-Miller
Managing Editor: Jack Kiburz
Project Editor: Trey Thoelcke
Interior Design: Lucy Jenkins
Cover Design: Design Alliance, Inc.
Typesetting: Elizabeth Pitts

Published by Upstart Publishing Company®,
a division of Dearborn Publishing Group, Inc.

Printed in the United States of America

01  10 9 8 7 6 5 4

Library of Congress Cataloging-in-Publication Data

Norman, Jan.
    What no one ever tells you about starting your own business / by
Jan Norman.
      p.   cm.
    Includes index.
    ISBN 1-57410-112-9
    1. New business enterprises—Management.   2. Entrepreneurship.
I. Title.
HD62.5.N68   1999
658'.041—dc21                             93-30479
                                              CIP

# DEDICATION

To my husband, Mark Landsbaum,
without whom this book would never have been written.

DEDICATION

# CONTENTS

# Part 3   The Money Chase 71

# Part 4   Management Issues 105

# Part 5   Helping Hand(s) 139

# Part 6    Marketing  171

# PREFACE

If you are thinking about starting a business—and even if you already have started one—this book is your opportunity to learn from those who went before you.

This also is a book of surprises—101 of them. One thing is for sure: The 101 business owners in this book wish *they* had known about these surprises in advance.

I asked hundreds of business owners this question: If you could start all over again, what would you do differently to be more successful, to be successful sooner, or to be successful with less effort? From their stories, I chose 101 to share with you.

This is your chance to benefit from their hindsight. When you've finished reading this book, you will know what they didn't when they started out.

These experiences are not flukes, nor are they isolated to certain industries or regions. The 101 people and businesses profiled in these pages are drawn from every region of the country, plus Guam. Their ventures touch every industrial category. The businesses range from one-person, home-based offices to billion-dollar global corporations. The youngest owner was in his early 20s when he began. The oldest was in his 60s. They are men and women, minorities and immigrants, the rich and the merely rich in spirit. Despite their diversity, they have much in common. And if you're a budding business owner, they share this bond with you, too.

Sooner or later (and probably more than once) you will be surprised by something you did not anticipate when you decided to go into business. Each of these people was. In fact, I've interviewed thousands of business owners in the past decade, and they all tell stories of being surprised after entering the wonderful world of entrepreneurship because they didn't expect—or no one ever told them about—*something*.

I'm certain you will find a useful tip, a helpful insight or at least a warning sign in these stories. In fact, I'm certain you will find more than one.

However, you won't learn everything about business ownership in these pages. Some stories may not relate to you or to your business directly, but if only one of the 101 is helpful, you just might be more successful (or successful sooner) or you might not have to work so hard at being successful than you would have otherwise. At least that's what each of these 101 business owners told me. (Imagine if 99 or 100 of these stories help you!)

Other than the fact that each person profiled here was surprised by the unknown, another undercurrent runs through all 101 stories. It is the irrepressible will to succeed—something seemingly so rare these days, yet nearly universal among successful business owners. Success did not come easily to any of these entrepreneurs. Each faced challenges; many faced multiple setbacks; some failed miserably before succeeding. But each had the will to press on, to achieve a dream, to reach a goal.

You will find that some of the 101 business owners solved their problems by doing the very things others found to be of no help at all. Circumstances and personal style will dictate what works for you, as they did for these business owners. For example, Jim Dartez thinks it would have been easier to give up some ownership in his company to get working capital, but Gia McNutt never would have considered such a thing. Patty Musich wishes she had started with a partner, but Roy Robbins regrets that he did. No magic wands or one-size-fits-all answers exist. Yet in this potpourri of wisdom and experience, you are bound to find something helpful.

When you do, don't thank me. Thank the people responsible: the 101 courageous souls who braved the harsh realities of commerce and emerged better for the experience. They are generous in spirit. They were happy to share their hard-learned lessons with me, and now with you, because in doing so they might help others travel that road more comfortably. My advice to you is this: take advantage of their gift.

I have arranged their stories in six parts. The first, "Look Before You Leap," relates how advance planning can avoid problems down the road. "Early Decisions" tells how critical threshold decision making is in starting a business. "The Money Chase" throws light on costs and sources of the green stuff. "Management Issues" gives rare insight into developing a boss's know-how and perspective. In "Helping Hand(s)," see where help awaits and how best to use it. The final part, "Marketing," underscores the importance of matching what you sell to what people want.

If you absolutely cannot tolerate the unexpected and shy away from challenges, you probably should not go into business for yourself. Successful business owners will tell you that surprises are the challenge, not the penalty. Learn from these veterans of the business world. Be forewarned and forearmed. When surprises surface, be ready to adjust and move forward. After all, the uncertainty of business ownership is a great part of its wonder—and it's fun.

# ACKNOWLEDGMENTS

I want to thank all of the business owners who took the time to tell me about the surprises they encountered and the lessons they learned when starting their companies, but especially those business owners featured in this book.

I couldn't have found these people without the help of the U.S. Small Business Administration, the 1996 White House Conference on Small Business, the Service Corps of Retired Executives—especially Betty Otte of the Orange County, California, chapter—and the Small Business Development Centers.

I am also grateful for the help of Judee Slack, Linda Pinson, and Denise Ross.

# AUTHOR'S NOTE

To business owners everywhere: I want to know about you.

You are a special breed. Those who follow in your footsteps can benefit greatly from your knowledge. No business owner has time to learn every lesson the hard way—by trial and error. By sharing the lessons that you have learned, together we can help those who follow to avoid unnecessary setbacks and even failure.

You can help by answering the following questions:

- What was the most surprising lesson you learned when starting, managing, and growing your business?
- If you were to do it all over again, what would you do differently?
- How might you have avoided setbacks, financial pitfalls, disappointments, and frustrations?
- What do you wish someone had told *you* about business ownership?

You can write to me at P.O. Box 5526, Diamond Bar, CA 91765-7526.
Or e-mail me at jannormanbiz@earthlink.net.
Or fax me at 909-860-5177.
Or visit my Web site at www.smallbusinessresources.com.
You have my best wishes for entrepreneurial success.

# PART 1

# LOOK BEFORE YOU LEAP

### ■ ■ ■

You've got this seed. Some people describe it as a burr, an itch, a gnawing idea, or a passion. You want to start some venture to scratch the itch or realize the passion.

No one ever told you how much planning you need, where the money should come from, how much you should know, or what to ask if you know you don't know. What the experts do tell you just may be wrong. Man! This business stuff is hard, but nobody ever told you how hard. And you haven't even hocked the house yet.

Before you run off and do something you'll regret, take a deep breath and think what you need to launch your enterprise successfully. If you lack the training and experience your particular venture requires, now is the time to get it. If you don't have enough information and market research to point you in the right direction, now is the time to get it.

Write—yes, *write*—a business plan. If that plan has some holes, ask one more question, study one more spreadsheet, look at one more possible location.

The pre-start-up phase is the time of greatest impatience for the new business owner. You're eager to run. Just be sure you know where the track is.

After you've prepared and have that sense that your idea and the timing are right, trust yourself to make it happen, even if the supposed experts can "prove" you're wrong. Now is the time to do it.

# 1. IT ALL STARTS WITH A DREAM

### Sometimes the conventional wisdom is wrong.

■ ■ ■

**A**nyone who watches American television knows that Dave Thomas is the world's biggest hamburger fan. The founder of Wendy's International appears in commercials for the 5,200-unit restaurant chain. Few customers realize, however, that Dave made his first million dollars as a Kentucky Fried Chicken franchisee. He even invented the rotating bucket sign that stood over thousands of KFC restaurants for years.

But when Dave sold his franchises at the age of 37, his dreams drifted back to his favorite food: hamburgers. Fresh meat, slowly grilled, in large proportion to the bun.

"Everyone told me—especially bankers and financial people—that opening another hamburger restaurant was a bad idea," Dave says. "They said the market was saturated. McDonald's and Burger King had all the business they could handle, and the world didn't need another hamburger restaurant."

If Dave had listened to the experts, he never would have launched the $6 billion Wendy's, named for one of his daughters.

Instead, Dave followed his instincts and his dream. On November 15, 1969, he opened a restaurant in Columbus, Ohio, that served made-to-order hamburgers, chili, french fries, thick milkshakes, and soft drinks. That was the entire menu. The first day, customers lined up out the door.

"The other guys sold batch-cooked hamburgers made from frozen beef that sat under a heat lamp," Dave says. "I knew that people would like what Wendy's offered. And, luckily, I was right."

Luck had little to do with it. If you're going to follow your instincts, you'd better hone them well first. Since age 13, when Dave began working in a restaurant, he talked about opening his own business some day. He learned every aspect of the business, from cleaning tables and flipping burgers to focusing the menu and marketing.

He may not have had a written business plan and formal market research, but Dave had been creating that plan and gathering information informally for 25 years.

"Research isn't everything," Dave wrote in his autobiography, *Dave's Way*. "Not long after we started, Burger King paid a lot of money for a research study that explained why Wendy's wouldn't work."

Wendy's did work, Dave says, because it provided what customers wanted—quality coupled with fast service. And Dave found that customers were willing to pay more for a good hamburger. Later, when customers asked for an expanded menu, Wendy's, now headquartered in Dublin, Ohio, added salads, baked potatoes, stuffed pita sandwiches, and chocolate chip cookies.

In the beginning, Dave's vision for Wendy's wasn't international. He even continued his executive job at another restaurant chain for awhile. Yet his first restaurant was profitable after six weeks. He opened a second one a year later. The chain expanded beyond Ohio in 1972. That's when he quit his other job.

"I'm often asked for advice about what it takes to start a business and make it a success," Dave says. "It all starts with a dream. The hardest part is being willing to do whatever it takes to make your dream a reality."

Dave has some basic rules for putting flesh and bones on a dream:

- Do your research. Know the business you want to start. Understand your customers and their needs.
- Your dream must be different in some way from your competitors' dreams.
- Quality and customer service must be your twin top priorities.
- You must work hard.

"If you don't have a burning desire to succeed, you won't," Dave emphasizes. "And when you do succeed, it's very important that you give back to your community."

# 2. MAKE A PLAN

A formal, written business plan serves an
invaluable, positive purpose for a new venture.

■ ■ ■

**P**atricia Creedon seemed destined to own an electrical contracting company. Her father was a construction manager for Dupont, and she married an electrician. Throughout her childhood, her father talked about starting a business, "and he brought me into his dream," Patricia recalls. "He always said, 'You can be president.' He gave me that entrepreneurial spirit."

Although he had sons, Patricia's father always shared his vision with her. Gender bias didn't exist for him.

When she did start Creedon Controls, Inc., in Wilmington, Delaware, in 1989, she was the president and Dad was vice president, even though he lived in another state. She relied heavily on his mentoring.

Patricia was so busy incorporating her company, writing the bylaws and running after customers that she didn't write a formal business plan.

"I had it in my head, but there's a big difference in putting it on paper," she says.

It was an oversight that almost sunk her fast-growing company.

She worked out of the basement in her home. The daily grind of growing a company while raising three children kept her from meeting with other entrepreneurs to share problems and concerns.

Despite double-digit annual sales growth, Creedon Controls was cash poor. After five years, Patricia thought she would lose her business.

"I had a good story to tell, but I didn't know it," she says. "I needed money and didn't know how to get it."

In the start-up phase, Patricia had attended a few workshops put on by the Service Corps of Retired Executives (SCORE), a business counseling group affiliated with the U.S. Small Business Administration. She returned to SCORE counselors to help her write her business plan.

A typical business plan consists of four sections, beginning with the statement of purpose: the company's objectives and why it will succeed. If the plan is used to obtain financing, this segment should state how much money the company needs, how the company will use the money, and how the company will repay the loan or compensate investors.

The business plan should include an organization section that describes what the company does and the distinctiveness of its products or services. Creedon Controls, for example, performs electrical contracting for heavy industrial uses, specializing in robotics and fiber optics. Patricia describes the qualifications and responsibilities for herself and her top executives. If she had written the plan when she founded her company, she would have detailed her start-up costs and her five-year plans. This section also should describe the company's system for maintaining financial and other records, all insurance, and security measures, such as inventory control.

The business plan's marketing section should describe the company's potential customers and how to reach them. It should evaluate direct and indirect competition and the company's competitive advantages. All promotional activities, pricing, packaging, and distribution also should be detailed in the marketing section. Finally, the business owner should use the marketing section to discuss industry trends and how the company will lead them.

The financial section summarizes the company's available capital and financial needs. A new company needs a pro forma cash flow statement and a three-year income projection using the revenue and spending information from the pro forma. This is the part new entrepreneurs hate: How can they know the dollars and cents until they're actually in business? That's where research of the industry and competition helps. Books, trade association publications, surveys, and studies contain financial information about similar companies that can serve as a guide.

The business plan is the blueprint, not the building. As circumstances change and new information and experience come to light, the plan can be changed.

Any documents—executives' resumes, financial analyses, leases, incorporation papers—used to write these four sections of the business plan should be placed in the plan's appendix.

"Writing a business plan got me out of the day-to-day grind and let me focus on the future," Patricia says. "Entrepreneurs need to spend time on the vision."

Her company now focuses on the high-tech end of electrical contracting. Creedon Controls installs fiber optics, heat tracing, and sophisticated security systems for offices and industrial plants, and robotics systems for manufacturers.

Patricia is now working on a strategic business plan for the future and is active in executive advisory boards, which hones her own skills while allowing her to work for good causes.

"I probably got into business at the worst time," she says of the early 1990s, which was marked by the nation's worst recession since the Great Depression. The construction industry was hurt severely. However, the discipline required to survive a poor economy helps an entrepreneur do even better in good economic times.

# 3. SUDDENLY, YOU'RE NOBODY

Line up plenty of cash and credit lines before
starting your business because you may
not be able to get them later.

■ ■ ■

Luciano Capote—his friends call him Lucky—knows what it's like to start with nothing. When he immigrated to Texas from Cuba in the 1950s, he was penniless and didn't speak a word of English. He washed dishes for two years and saved enough money to go to Texas A & M University. After he graduated, he got a job with a start-up computer company called Texas Instruments.

Lucky advanced as the company grew, and he eventually managed 400 employees. Lucky discovered that banks court corporate executives with offers of home equity loans and credit cards. Through these offers, Lucky had access to the funding he would eventually need to start his own company. But while still employed at Texas Instruments, Lucky did not know how difficult it would be to raise the money once he became self-employed. When he canceled a $50,000 home equity line of credit, it never occurred to him he was cutting off a source of money that would be next to impossible to find once he launched his own business.

At the age of 58, Lucky felt too dissatisfied to stay at Texas Instruments and too young to retire. So in 1984, Lucky took his retirement savings and started National Microcomp Services in the garage of his Tustin, California, home to service computer systems for corporations and public agencies. Prospects were excellent of winning contracts with companies that owned Texas Instrument computers but lacked in-house repair skills.

"I tried to get that line of credit back, and the banks wouldn't talk to me," Lucky says. "If you check that box that says 'Are you self-employed?' on the loan application, the computer will read nothing else."

He couldn't even get a line of credit at a large bank with which he had a $120,000 contract to service its automatic teller machines.

"People take for granted that they will get a line of credit because they own property, but the self-employed often can't unless they have personal relationships with their bankers."

Many would-be business owners think they'll get their money from banks, but most start-ups finance their dreams through Aunt Edna and the cookie jar—in other words, relatives and personal savings. A study by the National Federation for Independent Business (NFIB) in Washington, D.C., found that 75 percent of new businesses relied on their owners' money.

Lucky's cookie jar was his retirement money. Some business owners save for years or work two jobs. One business owner sold his coin collection. Another took a loan on his life insurance policy. Still another invested an inheritance. In the early 1990s, thousands of laid-off workers launched new ventures with their buy-out pay from their former employers.

The NFIB study found that almost a third of U.S. businesses receive a financial push from family and friends. Still other businesses turn to helpful suppliers and customers.

Don't let the lack of money hold you back, Lucky advises. Just as he managed to get a college education on minimal resources, he managed to grow Microcomp Services tenfold from his garage days to contracts and employees from Hawaii to Arizona. The company has had multimillion-dollar contracts to repair and service computer equipment for the Navy and for major corporations such as Motorola and Data General.

Lucky finally got that line of credit after almost five years by turning to a small local bank where the loan officers knew him well. However, to this day, he must sign his personal guarantee for business loans.

# 4. START WITH WHAT YOU KNOW

Choose a business you know and with
which you have experience.

■　■　■

**N**orris Randall, fresh out of the Army and holder of a college degree in industrial arts, had a job offer to teach high school. Then his father called for help.

Louie Randall had owned a successful men's clothing store, but in 1956, he was talked into starting a tile installation business by a guy with big promises: "We can make $100 a day building bathrooms, and we'll split it 50-50."

It was a business neither father nor son knew anything about. If Norris had stuck with his training, he would have gone into woodworking. He had, in fact, built several houses before his father's leap from retailing to tile work.

Louie bought a used pickup truck and some materials, then asked Norris if he'd like to learn the tile business from his expert partner.

"Big mistake," Norris admits. "It quickly became apparent that the man did not know much about business recordkeeping and the need to make a profit."

The partner, for example, didn't bother to figure the cost of materials and shipping into his pricing. After a few months, the tile man was gone, and Norris continued Randall Tile Co. in Phenix City, Alabama, learning on the job.

"It was still a seat-of-the-pants operation," Norris says. "I wouldn't do it that way again. I'd have chosen something I had some knowledge of and experience with."

After three years in business, Norris thought the company was doing well until an accountant friend helped him figure his income taxes.

"After we figured out that I had made $4,400 for the whole year, he said, 'You might as well go out and get a job.' That's when I realized this was not a game," Norris says.

Fortunately, Norris's wife had a nursing job to support the family.

That financial exercise was the wakeup call Norris needed to get a handle on each project's costs. In the past, when Norris bid for a job, the customer would claim that a competitor was willing to do the work for less. Norris would meet the lower price to get the work.

"I decided, if I can't make a profit, I don't want that job," he says.

He stopped meeting competitors' bids and stuck to his own terms. As Norris's reputation grew, customers started giving him the work anyway because of his quality, reliability, and references. Much later, Norris figured out that many of those lower bids were phantoms.

In 1960, after the birth of the Randalls' third son, Norris's wife quit her nursing job to keep the books for Randall Tile Co. Nine years later, the company stopped accepting installation work and concentrated on supplying tile and related materials to contractors. As a supplier with one location, Norris was better able to manage his workforce than he had been with dozens of work sites spread over a wide area.

Norris is semiretired now, and his son, James, runs Randall Tile Co.

Today, the five-employee company must compete with national warehouse retailers like Home Depot. The key, Norris says, is resisting the urge to meet competitors' prices.

"One of our biggest customers told my son that we don't have the lowest price, but the competitor couldn't guarantee he'd have the product, and we could," Norris says. "We always come to the rescue; that's how we survive."

# 5.

## SELF-TAUGHT

New business owners must do their own
market research. They must not rely on
other sources or government agencies,
whose goals are not their own.

■ ■ ■

After a career in Naval intelligence, Jack Givens started teaching international management to college business majors. He grouped students into teams to write business plans for companies exporting specific products to specific countries. The academic exercise was good training for international commerce, for which these students were preparing.

"I did my own homework, to find out what the students would encounter, and discovered that while the U.S. Department of Commerce had statistics, its employees didn't know much about running a business," Jack says. "I'd ask, 'Where am I going to sell my product?' and they'd say, 'Gee, we don't know. You have to tell us where you want to go and we'll give you information.'"

So he asked first about the Philippines because he had lived and worked there for several years. Jack found, based on his years of working all over the world, that much of the information he collected from the Department of Commerce about the Philippines and other countries was unverified or meaningless.

"I wouldn't base any business decision on one source, but with this kind of service from the government, a small business would go bankrupt," Jack says.

He carried that experience with him when he started InterTrade Systems, Inc., a Sandpoint, Idaho, company that trains U.S. small businesses in international trade. The firm's second mission is to show governments in developing countries how to create business incubators.

For starters, Jack sampled the assistance from numerous small-business agencies, organizations and volunteers and found that they were inadequate by themselves. The groups often drew upon studies, databases, and statistics collected by the government or academic groups. The data are plentiful, but must be interpreted and put into the context an individual company will face, Jack says. Numbers in a vacuum are meaningless, yet they're so voluminous that many entrepreneurs don't know where to start.

"Many small-business owners say they don't have time to do the research," Jack says. "But no one has the vested interest in your business success that you have. If you allow someone else to do your research, he won't challenge the information like you will, so the results and recommendations might not be the best for your particular company."

Jack found that he had to do the research for InterTrade himself. He knew the right follow-up questions to ask, pursued leads, and wouldn't give up when he got the runaround from federal bureaucrats.

Jack found that many American companies wouldn't pay for his research assistance in developing their international marketing plans. However, he did enter into contracts with the World Bank to create business incubators in developing countries. These countries then came to him for training in keeping these incubators going and growing.

Patience is an absolute necessity, Jack has discovered firsthand, because of the instability in developing countries. Mongolia, for example, has changed political leadership six times since he first started talking with country leaders about its business development efforts. He learned for himself that Mongolians don't answer the telephone if they're not expecting a call. An unsuspecting telemarketer would go nuts.

Jack's personal knowledge of international business proved invaluable as he tried to open doors in foreign markets. He always lets foreign dignitaries know that he is president and chairman of InterTrade, even though he makes it clear that the company is small.

"I'm asked to speak to business groups all over the world, but if I hadn't been this 'corporate chairman,' heads of state wouldn't talk to me," he says.

# 6.

## DON'T BUY BLINDLY

Investigate its finances thoroughly before
buying a business.

■ ■ ■

Celia Dorr knew it was time to change careers when she passed out from stress at the big law firm where she had worked for years. A friend of hers was equally in need of a change, so they marched blindly into business ownership.

"We thought that if we could buy a secretarial service, it would be easier because we would already have an established customer base," Celia says. "We would have the necessary equipment, and everything would be in place."

When Celia and her friend saw an advertisement for a secretarial service in a beach community 40 miles from their homes, they set out to buy it.

"We could envision ourselves having wonderful lunches overlooking the ocean, and we'd have a luxurious store-front office," Celia laughs.

The seller was asking $100,000 for the business and equipment, and Celia thought she was driving a hard bargain by offering $85,000.

"Thank goodness the business broker had ethics," she says, "because he advised us to make our offer based on the company's books and records."

Celia and her friend hired a business appraiser who first interviewed them about their goals, the services they wanted to offer, their experience, and their target market. Then he interviewed the business seller, inspected the equipment, and reviewed the company's finances.

He appraised the business's value at $15,000. The equipment was obsolete and no longer under warranty. It had no contracts to guarantee that a certain amount of work would remain with the company after the sale. The business was not making enough profit to support one business owner, he told them, let alone two.

"We were shocked!" Celia says. "We immediately rescinded our offer."

Many inexperienced entrepreneurs believe, as Celia did, that buying an existing business is less risky than starting from scratch. And a going concern does have some potential advantages, such as immediate revenue, location, established reputation, contracts, customers, inventory and equipment.

However, many established companies, like old houses, come with problems. A company's location may be on the decline. Its reputation may be bad. Its equipment may be obsolete, broken, or completely depreciated. And, as Celia discovered, the seller is likely to have an inflated view of the company's worth. While a company with patented products, strong management teams, and a strong competitive advantage can sell for many times its annual profit, a personal service business may sell for an amount equal to a year's profit or less.

As a prospective buyer, you can do some of the due diligence yourself. First, talk to business neighbors to find out potential problems with the location or the specific company. Also, you can learn a great deal just by hanging around and observing the location and the business at different times during the day. Be cautious about telling anyone you are a prospective buyer, however, because word about a pending sale can harm a business and expose you to a lawsuit by the seller.

Unless you understand financial records, hire an expert to examine the books of any company you are thinking about buying. Hire an attorney to review the sales contract.

"Our business appraiser charged us $1,500, and it was the best money I ever spent," Celia says. That appraiser recommended that Celia and her friend start their own secretarial service close to their homes instead of buying one.

Sterling Keystroke Services opened in Fullerton, California, in 1989. Celia's partner soon left because of personal problems, but Celia has expanded her secretarial services to include desktop publishing and resumé writing.

Over the years, Celia has had several owners offer to sell her their businesses. "Each time, I followed our appraiser's example. I reviewed the books and records, looked at the equipment that was for sale, determined what I was really buying, and, in the end, decided to buy only a portion of one business," she says.

# 7. WORK FOR FREE

Your learning curve will be shorter if you work
in the business or a similar one before you
buy or start your enterprise.

■ ■ ■

**J**eff Stark quit a management job with a national electronics retailer in 1989 to buy La Habra Moving and Storage in La Habra, California Jeff's work background brought invaluable experience to the company. As a manager in the large retail chain, Jeff learned to deal with employees; serve even difficult customers with a smile; and value computers in organizing and running a business.

"However, I had never worked for a moving business before purchasing one," Jeff says. "If I did it again, I would spend 90 days working for no salary under the tutelage of a mentor so that when I took the reins I would have hit the ground running. The way I did it, I'm sure it took me more than two years just to feel comfortable with all the ins and outs of the business."

Jeff chose to buy an existing company with a proven track record, a steady income stream, and a solid reputation for quality work; however, the business was worn around the edges. Jeff brought to La Habra Moving an infusion of enthusiasm, energy, and desire to grow the company. What he lacked was knowledge of the moving industry and understanding of his particular company's strengths and weaknesses. Learning these things while dealing with all the other issues of ownership took time away from expanding the company.

Over time, Jeff discovered that La Habra Moving offered services and products that even regular customers didn't know about. Imagine Jeff's dismay when he showed up for a moving job shortly after buying the company and learned that the customer had bought moving boxes from a competitor because she didn't realize La Habra Moving would not only sell her boxes, but deliver them.

Too many people think they want to own a restaurant because they love to cook or buy a flower shop because they love to garden. They don't appreciate how much of running a successful business has nothing to do with their passion. Some managers strike out on their own before they realize their previous jobs never trained them to handle financials, plan and execute marketing strategy, or clean the toilets at night if no one else does it.

Jeff thinks 90 days would have been enough to educate him in the details particular to the moving business. Perhaps. Some management experts recommend working at least a year in a business similar to the one you want to buy or start. Other successful entrepreneurs spend many years learning their crafts and industries before braving the wilds on their own. The time you spend working in a specific business before taking ownership has less to do with how fast you learn and more to do with your comfort level and past experience and the technicalities of the trade.

Despite his leap-before-training technique, Jeff did well with La Habra Moving. Under Jeff's management, the company increased revenues fivefold. Its staff increased from 4 to 25. He created a separate company, Box Connection, to sell moving supplies and deliver them to local customers. In 1997, he affiliated his local moving company with Wheaton Van Lines so he could accept interstate moving jobs, a requirement for further growth. But that growth wasn't what Jeff wanted for himself. He sold the moving company and kept Box Connection because Jeff felt that its potential for expansion is greater than the moving business's potential, while competition is less.

# *8.*    KNOW THE RULES

Before launching your business, learn
the laws and local ordinances that
affect your enterprise.

■ ■ ■

**J**anie Williams had worked for tax preparation companies for ten years when she decided to open her own tax and bookkeeping practice in her home in 1993. Imagine her surprise when she went to city hall to get a business license and learned that her municipality prohibits home-based tax preparation businesses.

Estimates of the number of home-based businesses range from 18 million to 47 million, depending on who's counting and what is being counted.

The technology—personal computers, software, telephone services, and more—that has fostered this growth of home-based businesses has expanded much faster than municipal government's ability and willingness to cope with the phenomenon. Some cities flat out prohibit businesses in the home; most have restrictions that limit the type of work that can be done from home. Even the tax laws are tougher on home-based businesses.

But Janie Williams' lesson applies to companies starting out in shopping centers, warehouses, or office buildings, too. Entrepreneurs should investigate zoning laws, lease restrictions, and property association rules before opening their businesses.

Janie says she is fortunate to live in Long Beach, California, which works with its business owners. Even though she made it clear she would be preparing taxes, the city listed Janie Williams & Associates only as a bookkeeping service, which Long Beach permits in residential neighborhoods.

Janie, who has become active in local and national home-based business groups, stresses that it is important for home-based business owners to be open and honest with governing entities. It is better to learn the limits in the beginning than to be shut down when an enterprise has contracts and obligations.

Janie is careful to abide by another city restriction that limits the number of clients who can visit a home-based business in one day. Many cities don't allow customer traffic, or even employee traffic, to homes, she says.

A friend of Janie had two employees working in his home business for two years without incident. Then he remodeled his kitchen. A city inspector checking on the construction noticed and reported the workers, and the city shut down the man's business.

Also, most cities don't allow home-based businesses to have signs.

"I wouldn't want one anyway," Janie says. "It announces to thieves that I have computer equipment on the premises."

Many of the restrictions imposed on businesses in the home are unfair because they don't apply to the same circumstances in which a business isn't present, Janie says. Many cities, for example, prohibit street parking for a business, but have no parking restrictions for houses with five or six adult and teenage drivers. They don't allow a business to have employees, but do allow a homeowner to have a full-time babysitter or housekeeper in the home. They don't allow home businesses to receive deliveries, but wouldn't dream of imposing such a restriction on mail-order shopping junkies.

"The laws vary widely across the country and in urban versus rural areas, so each business owner must find out for himself," Janie says. "Also, people who live in condominiums or planned communities have home-owner associations that often have more restrictive rules for home businesses than the cities do."

Many of the restrictions on home-based businesses have sound reasoning behind them. People don't want auto repair shops, toxic chemical plants, or all-night machine shops in quiet, residential neighborhoods. They don't want the streets packed with customers' cars or 12-foot-high neon signs blinking at night.

However, most cities don't have enough workers to run around looking for trouble, Janie says. They enforce their home business ordinances on the squeaky-wheel philosophy: if neighbors don't complain, business violations are ignored.

"It's important to know the rules, then not be too blatant if you can't abide by all of them," Janie says. "All my neighbors know what I do. They even come over on street-sweeping day to tell my clients they need to move their cars."

# *9.* DEVIL IN THE DETAILS

A new business owner needs both
big-picture vision and detail skills
to set up the infrastructure.

■ ■ ■

**A**fter a career in medical services and sales, Margot Adam Langstaff married, moved to Littleton, Colorado, and couldn't find a job. Finally, she started consulting for small businesses and, in 1992, created Financial Education Publishers, Inc., to develop and distribute financial materials designed to help small-business owners. Later, she added Oyster Communications to put financial products and services on the Internet for entrepreneurs and financial institutions. Among her products is a publication, "Small Business Financial Guide," and an online evaluation of a company's financial position.

"I know how to collect financial information. I know how to sell. I know how to market," Margot says. "What I didn't anticipate was the demand, especially by lawyers and financial people, that I know everything from the big picture to every line in my financial statements."

She found herself poring over paperwork at her desk one minute, then having to describe her grand vision the next. She felt that, especially as a woman, she always had to prove herself.

"It's grueling; you never get a break," she says.

The greatest help in learning how to see the big picture was getting a master's degree in business administration, Margot says.

"It taught me the level of sophistication of the people sitting across the negotiating table from me and what they expected of me," she says.

Learning to master the details took longer and was, for the most part, self-taught. The learning curve for new-business owners is sharp and pocked by mistakes that they must learn for themselves, Margot says.

"I had to set up the systems right away—bookkeeping, legal issues, infrastructure," Margot says. "I never would have anticipated that I would need all those skills."

Margot asked a woman entrepreneur who had started and sold a Fortune 500 company why she had been so successful. The woman responded, "I read everything that crosses my desk." It's a habit that Margot has cultivated, too, after an accountant caught a sizable mistake made by an attorney in a large licensing agreement. Margot hadn't read the agreement.

"I have read so many contracts, hundreds of them, and picked up large errors made by accountants and lawyers," she says. "It would have killed me if those documents had gone out."

Margot works with many contract workers who don't read the agreements before signing them.

"I find that very few people read contracts and financials, the grueling details that most of us would prefer to leave in that pile on the floor," she says. "The ability to concentrate on the details, even though we hate to do them, is crucial."

The key to business survival is never making the same mistake twice, she says. If Margot senses a problem heading her way—for example, in a negotiating meeting—she stops talking and listens. Then she goes home and researches the issue.

"I learn better if someone sits down with me and shows me the numbers," she says. "The financial side of business is more difficult for me because I wasn't an investment banker for years. I have been fortunate to have a group of people who, every step of the way, showed me how to do it."

An elderly business friend once told Margot the key to his wonderful life and successful career: anticipate.

"I asked, 'Anticipate crises? Things going wrong?' He smiled and said, 'Just anticipate.' So now I anticipate. And do the details."

# 10.

## FILL ME IN FULLY

If you buy an existing business, demand
complete operational information and
adequate training time from
the previous owner.

■ ■ ■

Lynette M. Smith owned a secretarial service in Yorba Linda, California, for 16 years. For 14 of those years, she was active in setting up and growing local and statewide networks of other services in her industry. She helped plan local conferences for the groups and wrote articles for an industry newsletter. She even wrote a book called *Starting a Successful Office Support Network.*

So it seemed like an easy transition when the owner of the National Association of Secretarial Services asked Lynette in 1996 if she wanted to buy the association. The United States is big on trade groups. *The Encyclopedia of Associations,* published by Gale Research in Chicago, lists more than 23,000 entries. While many are member-owned, board-run clubs, many others are for-profit businesses.

"I would have happily run my service until retirement, but when this offer came it was like I had been in training for it all along," Lynette says.

But the former owner wanted to sell quickly. As Lynette negotiated the deal, she kept copious notes on questions she wanted to ask later and ideas for improving operations. The potential seemed enormous. While the United States has 20,000 business support services, this association had fewer than a thousand of them. And it was the only national trade group in the industry.

"Unfortunately, the contract was signed only two weeks before owner-ship was transferred," Lynette says. "Only the second week was dedicated to training."

Her greatest need was more incubation time before the actual start-up at the new headquarters.

Like Lynette, so many new business owners discover surprises in their ventures despite their best efforts to prepare, educate themselves, and plan for all contingencies. Those who buy existing businesses often find the former owners less than enthusiastic, even if continued participation for one to five years is negotiated into a deal. Lynette wisely used the services of a business valuation expert, who uncovered many features about the business side of the association that Lynette would not have thought of. And her professional background made her more aware of problems and potential than an inexperienced buyer would be.

When Lynette took the association reins, it was losing membership. Less than half the affiliates renewed when their memberships expired. Few members knew that the association sold useful publications, an important profit center. Worse yet, Lynette didn't know about the royalty agreements for some of these publications.

To compensate for her lack of preownership training, Lynette worked 70 hours a week. She consulted with trusted members of the organization. She sought comments and suggestions from members, both current and lapsed. She added a Web site so potential members could find the associa-tion when they were surfing for advice. She followed up renewal notices with phone calls to those who let their memberships lapse. She updated publications and added new ones. She stressed the benefits of belonging to the group, such as free business consultations by phone, that members didn't even know they had. She pursued major corporate sponsors and encouraged new local chapters.

And when members said they didn't like the term "secretarial" in the association's name, Lynette changed it to the Association of Business Support Services, Inc.

The number of local chapters increased by more than a third in two years. Membership grew beyond a thousand and, more importantly, reten-tion of current members improved to 72 percent.

How much of this work would have been necessary anyway? Who knows? But Lynette's dream of 50-hour work weeks were further in her future than she imagined before buying the association.

# 11. OVERCOME IGNORANCE WITH DESIRE

### If you don't have experience or business know-how, you'd better want success enough to compensate.

■ ■ ■

Craig Hartman was still in high school when he started painting houses and decided he liked it enough to make a career of it. Not one to work for someone else, Craig started his own company, Preferred Industrial Services, Inc., in Fort Wayne, Indiana, in 1973.

Never mind that he had no experience running a business. Never mind that he had no technical knowledge. Never mind that his dad and adult friends told him to go to college instead.

"I talked to more than a hundred people during my start-up period," Craig says, "and most of them told me not to do it, I was too young, too inexperienced. I remember only four saying 'do it.'"

Craig ignored his doubters, but faced enormous barriers that he overcame only through an absolute refusal to fail and, as Winston Churchill put it, "blood, sweat, toil and tears."

"Without question, my lack of abilities in technical knowledge and business management significantly impeded my company's growth," says Craig, who resigned as Preferred Industrial Services president in 1998 to start a bank. "You need to have at least a solid foundation of business knowledge or experience so you know what it takes to run a business."

Craig's willingness to ask a hundred business people for advice helped him overcome his inexperience. Even those who urged him to go to college instead of start a business gave him plenty of helpful information.

But asking for help was tough. "Type A personalities don't like to admit they don't know everything," Craig says. "I had to make an honest assessment of where I was, a practice that has served me well over the years."

Craig hired workers and outside consultants to fill in the gaps in his knowledge and experience. One old hand taught him how to price jobs. Others taught him the differences in types of paint.

"Fortunately, I had solid sales skills," he says, "but the toughest sale was to get people to come to work for someone who was younger and dumber than they were."

Preferred Industrial Services expanded beyond house painting to replacing floors and roofs and repainting factories in 18 states east of the Mississippi River. His staff grew to 300 people. Annual sales exceeded $25 million.

But that growth wasn't without trauma. In 1980, Preferred Industrial Services was losing so much money on a government contract to paint bridges that Craig's accountant advised him to file bankruptcy. Instead, he persuaded his creditors to work with him to keep the company going. "To file bankruptcy wouldn't fit my M.O.," he says.

Only four creditors wouldn't cooperate. He paid them in full and swore never to do business with them again. No one lost a dime, and Preferred Industrial Services came roaring back.

However, in 1990, the company was in financial straits again. Craig had to sell stock to outsiders for the first time to save the company. He bought out these investors by 1997.

In 1998, Craig broke Preferred Industrial Services into four corporations. He retained minority ownership in three of them and sold what remained.

"You never stop learning in business," Craig says. "I have a solid foundation of business knowledge and expertise now, and most of the concepts are universal. I wouldn't expect [the learning curve] in my new venture to be to the degree it was the first time around. But no doubt five years from now, I'll have a laundry list of things I'd do differently."

# 12.   KNOW YOURSELF

The first-time business owner must recognize
and apply previously learned skills and life
experiences to the new venture.

■ ■ ■

Ellen Kruskie's careers as an employee and a business owner couldn't be much farther apart. As an employee, she held administrative jobs in medical practices and a biomedical start-up company. When she was laid off—and determined never to allow that to happen again—Ellen started a dog wash service.

Many entrepreneurs don't attempt such a dramatic change in gears. But Ellen didn't concentrate on the differences; she culled her working career for parts and tools that would make Carolina PetSpace in Raleigh, North Carolina, successful.

PetSpace is a do-it-yourself dog wash and accessories boutique specializing in dogs and cats. She likes to say she's been in business 24 years. Dog years. (She opened in 1994.)

"While my professional background was in a totally unrelated arena, basic business principles are the same. I don't care if you're running a high-tech company or a dog wash," Ellen says. "Everything you've ever learned or experienced applies."

Before launching her new company, Ellen assessed her background and realized that dealing with people was what she had enjoyed most about working in doctors' offices.

"Working one on one with customers at Carolina PetSpace is great," she says. "They don't just come in here, wash their dogs, and leave. Everyone has a problem. I'm a problem solver. It's not that different from working with patients in a doctor's office."

Being the biomedical start-up's first employee taught Ellen a lot about launching a new company of any type.

For the biomedical company, Ellen wrote a business plan that was two-and-a-half inches thick. The plan for PetSpace was 17 pages. She helped find multimillion-dollar funding and 7,000 square feet of industrial space for the biomedical start-up. That experience helped her finance and successfully negotiate a 2,000 square-foot retail shop for PetSpace.

Ellen thoroughly researched the shop's location and talked with everyone she could about the pet industry. "I knew what to look for. I knew the questions to ask," she says. "I just had to reapply the training."

Marketing the two businesses has been quite different, Ellen adds. One focused on attracting venture capital and building scientific credibility for two years before opening its doors. The other sells products, services, and advice direct to consumers.

Ellen's initial plan for PetSpace was to dedicate seven to nine months to research, planning, and construction before opening.

"However, the best laid plans can be thwarted by circumstances beyond one's control," she says. "My prep period stretched to nearly 16 months before the doors opened. The preplanning paid off in that while these delays were not desirable, either economically or personally, they were not disastrous either. And the time warp truly tested my resolve."

A business owner in any industry must be ready to adjust to the unexpected, Ellen says. But "anticipating and being prepared to accommodate a worst-case scenario for the proposed business eliminates a lot of unpleasant surprises," she adds.

When personal experience and skills don't supply an answer, go out and find it, Ellen says. About five months after opening PetSpace, she had the opportunity to buy a complementary business. Her previous employers had never contemplated an expansion, so Ellen had no idea how to evaluate the venture. Ellen sought the assistance of the Service Corps of Retired Executives (SCORE), whose volunteer counselors assist would-be and existing business owners. SCORE's expert advice helped Ellen see that the purchase was unwise.

She has now added the experience to her reservoir of knowledge, to be drawn upon in the future.

# 13.   HOBBIES AREN'T BUSINESSES

Without forethought or planning, a business
owner's appetite for more equipment and
space can easily eat up all the profits.

■ ■ ■

**W**hat could be more fun than making chocolate? It was Patricia Green's favorite hobby. Therefore, in 1980, she and a friend decided to teach a few candy-making classes and sell supplies.

They called their venture The Chocolate Tree. They leased a small industrial space off the beaten path; the landlord said they wouldn't last five months.

Patricia and her friend set up a display case housing samples of the candy students could learn to make, but customers continually came in and bought the samples. They had to make more samples constantly, and soon they were out of the hobby business and into manufacturing and retailing. They didn't realize it, however, because they hadn't thought through what they were doing.

They continued their hobby ways for a long time. In fact, they hand-dipped pieces of chocolate for two years.

"We just went on a wing and a prayer," Patricia laughs. "Consequently, it took forever to take money out of the business."

Something always gobbled up the money faster than Patricia could write herself a paycheck. For example, The Chocolate Tree needed more space to accommodate the growing number of orders, so Patricia bought an adjacent building, a former drive-through bank. Later, the company bought another bigger building, and Patricia and her whole family practically lived in the factory for months while they added electricity and water.

Also, lack of planning caused mistakes. Patricia once bought a 26-foot-long machine that was larger than either building she owned.

"Everything we earned we had to put into buildings or equipment. We should have thought it out more carefully," Patricia says.

But she wouldn't advocate this growth-without-planning approach to most start-up businesses.

"If the Small Business Administration's Small Business Development Center had been in existence in 1980, I would have had them help me with a business plan before opening," Patricia says. "When you have to pay off debts and reinvest everything in the business, it takes much too long to make a paycheck, even a small one."

Many hobbyists who try to turn their crafts into businesses encounter problems. Customers won't pay enough for a finished product to make a business profitable. Large-scale production is difficult to establish. Tasks that were fun on the weekend become grinding chores on a full-time basis. Or, worst of all, an owner might be so busy with management and marketing that she never gets to participate in the craft she loves.

The Chocolate Tree managed to outgrow its hobby roots without bankrupting the owners.

"Turning the tide simply took time—time to get equipment paid off, build inventory, and become known," Patricia says.

The Chocolate Tree benefited from serendipity that few small businesses stumble into. The company is located in Beaufort, South Carolina, where the movie *Forrest Gump* was filmed. The shop is not far from the spot where the Tom Hanks character philosophized that life is like a box of chocolates. The tie-in is not lost on tourists—or Hollywood. A team from the Nickelodeon cable channel came to town a few years ago and filmed a segment in The Chocolate Tree.

Today, The Chocolate Tree employs 12 people who make candy year round. In addition to maintaining the retail store and a mail-order business, the company wholesales chocolate to other retailers. Patricia still teaches chocolate-making classes and sells candy-making supplies to customers who are content to remain hobbyists.

# 14.

## SET YOUR SITES

Spend a little more, if necessary, to get the
right location for your business.

■ ■ ■

Chris McIntyre and Jeffery Brown, coworkers at an international corporation, dreamed of touring Europe on Harley-Davidson motorcycles. But before they could schedule the flight, the dream vacation evolved into the dream business. Chris and Jeff decided to rent Harley-Davidson motorcycles to European tourists in the United States; therefore, they started EagleRider Motorcycle Rental USA in Torrance, California, in 1992.

"When we first opened, there was no immediate need for a prime location because we were marketing overseas and our bookings came through travel agents," Chris says.

But the European tourist market proved to be seasonal, so Chris and Jeff started filling the gaps by marketing to Americans.

"Now we needed a higher visibility location," Chris says. "We should have spent more money on rent to secure a more prominent business location."

Location can be a make-or-break decision for many types of businesses. Retailers and others like EagleRider that depend on customers finding them need high visibility with adequate parking. Labor-intensive companies, like check processors, need to be near large labor pools. Manufacturers must be located close to highways, rail lines, or ports.

Fledgling business owners should evaluate their businesses before even looking for a site. They need to consider their target market—who their customers are and where they're located; whether their customers need to find them; who their competitors are and where they're located; how much space they need; and whether big signs are important.

Chris and Jeff decided EagleRider had to be within ten minutes of international airports in major foreign tourist destinations. The company currently has a fleet of 150 motorcycles in Los Angeles, San Francisco, Denver, Chicago, Las Vegas and Orlando. Both the Denver and Orlando locations are on the main roads between the airports and the downtowns. The Chicago operation is open just six months a year because of the city's harsh winters, so it's located in a major seller of Harley-Davidson products and accessories. The alliance benefits both.

The San Francisco office is tucked away on a side street in the downtown area. EagleRider has looked for a better location for more than a year, but "a location with visibility and good price is hard to find in San Francisco," Chris says.

And although Chris advocates spending more rent to get a prime location, he sets limits. The Las Vegas office is a block off the Strip, where the major casinos sit. One block means the difference between $2-a-square-foot rent and $10 or $15, he says. The new entrepreneur must balance the best possible choice with the business's budget.

All of EagleRider's locations cater mostly to men in their 30s with high disposable incomes. Whether Americans or Europeans, these renters belong to the passionate following the Harley-Davidson company has successfully cultivated for its high-performance motorcycles. They pay as much as $185 a day to ride their dream bike.

But the two customer groups are quite different, Chris says. For Europeans, riding motorcycles is a way of life. Their rentals are longer—ten days to two weeks. For Americans, riding a Harley is a dream fulfillment just for the weekend.

Although EagleRider offers several guided excursions, such as the "Outlaw Trails of the Wild West" tour through California, Utah, and Arizona, most Harley-Davidson renters prefer to escape on their own paths and timetables.

EagleRider confines its locations to major tourist destinations, which should still fulfill Chris and Jeff's long-term plan to grow the company to the largest motorcycle rental and tour company in the world.

But they still haven't taken that European vacation.

# *15.*        ## SO LITTLE TIME

The rapidity of change in the world has
shortened the time you have to make
your business successful.

■ ■ ■

**D**uring the 20th century, virtually every aspect of American life has accelerated, from car speed to global financial transactions. That speed is no friend of today's entrepreneur. Today, the United States has half the productive farms it had when Russ Brown started working for his dad, Larry Brown, in the mid-1950s. That means their company, AGSCO, in Grand Forks, North Dakota, which creates, manufactures, and distributes crop protection chemicals, has half the market with no comparable lessening of competition.

"It used to be said that you needed at least three years to bring a new business into the black," Russ says. "Today, you probably don't have more than two years, under most circumstances, to either succeed or fail."

While every person starting a new business should anticipate and plan, rapid change can negate the most carefully laid plans. Today's business owner must be willing to alter his plans quickly when necessary, Russ says.

Larry Brown started selling crops for his farmer employer during the Great Depression before launching his own business, AGSCO, in 1934. AGSCO had to adjust to accelerating technological developments and consolidation at every level from farm to retailer, says Russ, now chairman of AGSCO's board. Today, AGSCO has evolved into a product and service supplier to wheat and row crop farmers in five states and Canada.

Products AGSCO used to sell have been banned for environmental concerns, requiring the development of new and safer products and work methods. To replace the banned products, AGSCO created a division to design new products and methods to reduce their negative impact on the environment and economy. For example, the company developed sealed, returnable containers that set a new standard in chemical handling.

Too much fertilization is as much a problem as too little; therefore, the company now uses satellites to analyze land to determine that different amounts of fertilizer can be applied to different areas of the same field. AGSCO also supplies the machinery to apply the fertilizer with precision.

AGSCO also built a regional distribution and production plant near Grand Forks run by computers and protected by a state-of-the-art fire prevention system. As a young business owner, Larry Brown couldn't have envisioned such technology.

At the same time, farms, manufacturers, and retailers are buying out their competitors, forcing AGSCO to change its selling habits.

"Today, we sell very little through dealers; we sell direct to customers," Russ explains. "We haven't grown through acquisition, so it has become highly competitive. The pie keeps getting smaller on the customer side, but the competition doesn't let up. You can't take your foot off the accelerator."

AGSCO's sales exceed $26 million, and the third generation of Browns help run the company.

The rapidity of technological change and customer consolidation is tough on old-time companies, but even tougher on new ventures. Financial backers aren't as patient today, Russ says, and competitors breathe down your neck.

Time is not on the start-up's side.

"If I were starting now, I would look to develop partnerships and joint ventures as quickly as it could make sense," Russ says. "Do this not just on the sales and marketing side, but look to combine your cost centers with other businesses, also."

This approach enables the entrepreneur to multiply his efforts without giving up his status as an independent business, Russ says.

"The trick is to see these changes coming and be innovative in response," Russ advises.

# 16. HARDER THAN HARD

No one can fully prepare you for how
hard it is to run a business.

■ ■ ■

Laurey Masterton grew up in an entrepreneurial family. Her parents owned the Blueberry Hill Inn in Goshen, Vermont, in the early 1960s. Her two sisters—an attorney and a computer consultant—own their own businesses. And Laurey owned a commercial interior design firm that decorated showrooms for Hasbro Toys before starting Laurey's Catering and Gourmet-to-Go in Asheville, North Carolina, in 1987.

"We all skipped out of the corporate scene," Laurey says. Yet with all that business exposure, she continues, "It is really a whole lot harder than I thought it would be. I didn't know catering wasn't going to be the easiest thing. I didn't have a clue, and it's probably a good thing that I didn't."

Of all the challenges that entrepreneurs face, nothing matches in difficulty the everydayness of business ownership. It exists from the moment you wake up until the moment you collapse in exhaustion at the end of the day. It's exhilarating, terrifying, and constant.

"I think that the biggest challenge is keeping my spirits up," Laurey says. "I have averaged 30 percent growth for the past five years and still worry. I have never done better than my business did last year, and yet in a slower time of year, I find myself back in the worry mode."

Her background helps get her through the down times.

Laurey started her catering business in the kitchen of her second floor apartment. She had grown up around food, so the business was a return to her roots and a tribute to her mother, who died when Laurey was 12 years old.

"I couldn't go back and buy the inn [my parents owned], but I could do my own thing," she says.

She learned about business plans, taxes, word-of-mouth advertising, and networking through the Service Corps of Retired Executives.

"I created a single-page brochure, went to a local women's networking meeting, and introduced myself as a caterer, even though I did not know *what* I was talking about," Laurey says.

She volunteered to cater the group's next meeting. She also placed an ad in the group's newsletter, which brought the first contract, a party for Steelcase, Inc., a maker of office furniture. Many of the group's members remain regular clients and Steelcase continues to be a major account ten years later.

In the middle of her second year in business, Laurey was diagnosed with ovarian cancer. About the same time as she underwent treatment, she had to take out a large personal loan to pay taxes she hadn't expected. Shaken, but determined and hopeful, she returned to work as soon as she could.

As the business grew, Laurey realized she couldn't continue to run the company from her apartment. A private investor, Dana Smith, invested in

Laurey's Catering, bringing money, management expertise, emotional support, and down-to-earth advice. They incorporated the company and built a commercial kitchen.

Dana asked Laurey to make him dinners that he could pick up on his way home each night. That request led to Gourmet-to-Go, which grew to sell hundreds of gourmet dinners each week.

Laurey's Catering has grown to a 2,500-square-foot kitchen and gourmet shop that sells sandwiches and salads. The 12-employee company handles everything from intimate gourmet dinners to company picnics for 2,500 people.

"I could have chosen something easier, but I'm glad I took this challenge," Laurey says. "I really feel that the success of this business is something I earned, not something that fell into my lap.

"You have to be your own worst critic and your own best cheerleader," she adds. "Every business owner reaches a point when no one will be there telling you 'you can do it; you can do it.' You have to say that yourself."

# 17. PLAN FOR FAILURE

Failure *can* happen, so a business owner
must anticipate it with worst-case
scenarios when planning.

■ ■ ■

In 1982, Gerald Brong resigned his professorship at Washington State University to open Community Computer Centers, a value-added reseller of Kaypro computers. Within two years, the university was his major competition and dominated the market. As a nonprofit exempt from certain business and income taxes, the University could beat Gerald's prices. Gerald put too much money into inventory for a brand that was a loser in the computer wars. His business went bankrupt.

In the bright-eyed days before opening their ventures, too few business owners allow themselves to think about the possibility of failure. Gerald believes he should have built into his vision an escape plan in case something went wrong. With a worst-case scenario in hand, Gerald could have taken businesslike action to close the company before every dime of his savings and retirement funds were gone.

Although the federal bankruptcy system is designed to give individuals and business owners a fresh start, don't let anyone tell you bankruptcy is the easy way out. Reestablishing credit and savings can take years.

After filing for bankruptcy, Gerald and his wife, Marlene, had no assets, credit cards, or health insurance. They owed back taxes that were not discharged in the bankruptcy, plus 24 percent penalties and interest on those taxes. Gerald couldn't get his old teaching job back because his company had competed with the university's venture.

"We lost friends. They were embarrassed. They didn't want to hear about my failure," Gerald says.

The Brong family rebuilt its business one brick at a time.

"Having hit the bottom of the barrel and bounced around in the slop, there were only two things to do: Either drown in the slop or get out of the barrel," Gerald says. "Drowning didn't seem like an acceptable option."

The Brongs began by writing a business plan for their new business, which they named GMB Partnership. Gerald does writing, speaking, consulting, and training.

One of Gerald's rules for this new venture is that it does not require any up-front cash or keep any inventory. For example, if a client hires Gerald to assemble a computer system, the client buys the equipment first.

"In finding self-employment following failure, I developed business activities that conserve cash, leverage capital, and use intangible assets to generate positive cash flow," Gerald says. "I sold intellect, ideas, and available human time."

The Brongs decided to return to the Kittitas Valley in Washington State, where they married. "There's a good university library here," Gerald says. Plus, "The rural community doesn't judge people on their trappings."

That's helpful when you don't have many trappings.

Vacations consist of picnics in the backyard of their rented house. For entertainment, the family attends $3 concerts at the nearby university. After the bankruptcy, Gerald couldn't even rent a car when he went on business trips because he didn't have a credit card. However, he had kept his membership in Rotary International, and a fellow member, a bank manager, eventually cosigned for a credit card.

"We're aggressively working to reestablish our retirement funds, but my best guess is we will continue this lifestyle [and] I will continue to work well beyond 65," says Gerald, now 59 years old.

"Though there was frequently the 'I give up' response, it became obvious that giving up wasn't as much fun as survival."

# *18.*  GET OFF THE DIME

### Eventually, you have to quit planning
### and start the business.

■ ■ ■

**A**fter years in sales and training for international corporations, Larry Dybis launched his own business. Actually, he was given a shove. He did such a good job setting up a company's marketing program, the boss decided he didn't need anyone to run it. Larry was out of a job.

"I had been building up other companies for years," Larry says. "I decided, this time I will do it for myself." So, in 1995, Larry began People Dynamics in Western Springs, Illinois, a firm dedicated to strategic planning, training, and career coaching.

In a way, Larry was doing what he sees so many of his clients do: procrastinating. Procrastination is a symptom of uncertainty and fear. The would-be business owner spends excessive amounts of time finding an office, looking for furniture, and investigating multiple phone lines.

"I should have spent less time getting ready," Larry says. "Not that a person should not know what to do and how to do it, but overpreparing with excessive focus on 'I must know more, practice more, organize more' only delays your natural ramp-up time."

A new business requires a year or two to become established, pay its dues, and gain recognition among potential clients, he says. "Delaying this for any reason just makes the process more difficult and harder to endure."

One simple aid is to set a deadline for starting the business and stick to it, even if you haven't completed every task on your to-do list. Another is to slice off a small piece of the whole project and complete it. Or try the sneak attack. Do a task immediately before your mind has time to resist. Force yourself to put the most unpleasant task first. Once that's done, many of the fun parts of business start-up will flow.

Larry says he now recognizes these delaying tactics in many of his clients who want to start professional speaking or seminar practices.

"They don't want to be humiliated by delivering less than their best quality or value that they promised, so they work endlessly on their businesses," he says. "I tell them they have a tremendous amount of potential, but they must work to make sure it's not permanent potential."

Larry urges these clients to go out and give speeches for free. They don't have to have three-day seminars in hand to do that, he says.

"Give it away. That's how you establish connections and reputation; then build on it," he advises. "You need a feedback system to keep going. When you see the light bulbs go on while you're speaking, and people come up afterward and thank you, that validates your work."

Many entrepreneurs encounter resistance to their prices when trying to get their first clients. Larry suggests charging on an escalating scale. Charge your standard price, say $1,000, and give the client a $500 gift certificate. The understanding is that if the client recognizes the value of your work, the next project or program will cost $750, then $900, and finally your $1,000 standard fee.

"You're ramping yourself up, not just giving it away," Larry explains. "But do this only with someone who could become a good client."

"I have a friend who describes it this way: He says he's willing to polish a diamond in the rough, but he doesn't polish bricks," Larry says. "Some people just aren't worth this approach."

Regardless of preparation and planning, the final plunge into business ownership requires commitment, Larry says. "Don't tell yourself you're going to give it a year and see if it works out. Go after it completely, and success becomes a matter of time."

# TIPS . . .

1. If your research and experience tell you a business idea is a winner, don't worry about conventional wisdom.

2. Avoid the temptation to launch your venture with inadequate planning.

3. Arrange for home equity loans and credit cards before you leave your corporate job for self-employment.

4. When deciding what type of business to go into, look first at your skills and experience.

5. Do your own legwork so you will understand your new venture and its market.

6. Kick the tires, look in the trunk, and hire professionals to study the financials before buying a business.

7. Try out a business before you buy it.

8. Ask city, county, state, and federal officials about any laws or licensing that apply to your business.

9. Have a clear vision of the business you will build, but also be able to describe the nails, boards, and varnish.

10. Take your time in asking questions and learning the details of an existing business before closing escrow. Make the seller commit in writing to providing assistance for one to three years.

11. Take a gut check. Just how badly do you want this venture to succeed, and how much of yourself will you invest to make it happen?

12. Know your strengths. They're bound to help your new business succeed.

**13.** Sure, you want your new business to be fun, but planning before acting will help you enjoy it even more and keep you solvent.

**14.** The best location combines visibility, affordability, and lease terms you can live with.

**15.** Move quickly. Procrastination is a modern business killer.

**16.** If you want an easy job, don't start your own business.

**17.** Once you've envisioned the worst that could possibly happen, you are better able to adjust before disaster strikes.

**18.** Your business just might be the solution to someone's greatest problem. So get started.

# PART 2

# EARLY DECISIONS

■ ■ ■

The most frightening period for the new entrepreneur is not the prestart-up phase. That's fantasy time. The reality of small-business ownership sets in after you have made the commitment. The early decisions, once you're sailing the entrepreneurial seas, set the course.

New business owners tend to ignore the future consequences of their actions or inaction. Perhaps the most important task during the early days is to tune your attitude. Expect a positive outcome. Thicken your skin. Avoid reading evil motives into every adverse occurrence.

Adopt a posture of consistent persistence.

Like most new business owners, you might want to grab every customer who crosses your path, fearful another might never come along. Later, you will develop confidence that your products or services really do have value in the marketplace. Then you will weed out the losers, the late payers, and the complainers.

Like most new business owners, you might begin by offering too many products and services, again fearful that you won't make a living if you focus too sharply. Later, your confidence will allow you to dump the unprofitable lines. Lo and behold, you'll be even more profitable. You wouldn't have believed it at first.

Occasionally, you probably will concentrate so hard on doing the two-step that you'll miss some embellishments that could waltz you right into the big time.

# 19. THE SUPPORTS ARE GONE

New business owners who are corporate
refugees don't realize how much they relied on
their old workplaces for validation, services,
interaction, and emotional support.

■ ■ ■

Tracey Campbell was a financial journalist and market prognosticator
for Market Scope, the wire service of Standard and Poor's. Her husband
dreamed of owning his own business, but lacked the "swing from the chandelier and leap" personality, as Tracey puts it. So, in 1995, she leaped
instead, creating 1-888-Inn-Seek, a 24-hour telephone and Internet service
set up to search for bed-and-breakfast inns throughout the United States.
The company is headquartered in her Danbury, Connecticut, home.

If you're one of those corporate dwellers whose company is heartless,
whose boss is a jerk, whose coworkers are strangers, and whose job is joyless, think twice about chucking it all for your own business, Tracey says.

"I took for granted the infrastructure built into my job," she remembers.
"The office supply closet was always stocked. Information Services was
always there to fix my computer."

Tracey operates 1-888-Inn-Seek from a farmhouse that is 264 years old,
give or take a few decades. If Tracey runs out of envelopes, she runs to the
store. If her computer breaks down, she spends hours on the telephone, holding for the manufacturer's technical support line, or she spends the afternoon
traveling back and forth to the nearest computer store. She has rebuilt her
computer server twice. All three hard drives crashed simultaneously.

When a potential client asked for a brochure, she had to create her
own. And when she ordered 10,000 tent business cards, she had to fold
them herself.

The psychological side is equally important.

"There is something about getting a paycheck that validates what you
do," Tracey says. "You write a memo and it goes someplace and people read
it. I used to do a lot of television and radio appearances, so I got some fan
mail.

"I've never thought of myself as an egomaniac, so I never thought I would miss all that."

To combat her isolation and lack of experience, Tracey started a Web Girls chapter, which provides support for women learning computers and technology. To avoid bogging down in a sea of menial tasks sucking away her limited time, she found a nearby sheltered workshop that charged just $10 for every thousand business cards folded and tied with ribbon into bundles of ten. The computers will always be a challenge, but Tracey has learned to do some of her own programming and local networking.

1-888-Inn-Seek originally was going to fax information back to callers, but Tracey couldn't find satisfactory software. Instead, callers can search the database of inns by using a touch-tone phone. The same information can be searched many ways on the Web site, which gets 2,000 visitors a day. Visitors can search by location, amenities, or special events. They can find inns that allow pets. They can search for an inn near a friend's home by entering the friend's telephone number. Some innkeepers and event planners pay to add descriptions of their offerings to the phone service and Web site.

As Tracey discovers more sources of help and information, learns to handle tasks once left to corporate assistants, and expands marketing avenues, her memories of corporate support dim.

But she still hasn't found anyone to read her memos.

# 20. THE VALUE OF FIRST

Duplicating what someone already provides
in a niche market is a loser's formula.
Find your own niche.

■ ■ ■

**B**ud Blackburn was a farmer and jack-of-all-trades when his Uncle Ray, a land surveyor, came to him with an idea. In the 1940s, surveyors used heavy lath sticks to mark their work. Ray thought a lighter weight flag would be more efficient. Bud spent about four years developing, in his spare time, a machine to produce the flags, and in 1953 he opened Blackburn Manufacturing with his father and uncle on the family farm south of Royal, Nebraska.

It would have been futile for the Blackburns to copy the lath sticks already in use, says Bud's son, Jim, president of the company since 1980. To survive and thrive, a small company must be first and different. "Me-too-ism" is a killer.

"I believe our company's success can be attributed to being the first company to introduce this niche product," Jim says.

Blackburn Manufacturing's first customers were soil and water conservation districts that needed markers for laying out terraces that prevent erosion. The Blackburns refused to go into debt to start their little venture. Still, demand grew steadily. After four years, the company was selling so many flags that Bud sold the farm and went into flag making full time.

Jim, who grew up in the business, remembers helping on the first million-flag order when he was a boy. After a stint in the Navy, Jim joined the company full time in 1973. At the same time, Bill Lawson became a partner, bringing with him a process of silk screening names and labels onto the flags. This process opened the specialty product to a new market, utility companies. Blackburn Manufacturing adapted the utilities' color coding, such as red flags to mark electrical lines and green flags for sewer pipes.

"Considering the business environment in the 1950s and 1960s, I believe the slow and steady growth of the business combined with zero indebtedness are primary factors in our business success. It was especially beneficial in the 1980s, with interest rates and inflation in the double digits."

The flags certainly were not glamorous, but they were so useful and inexpensive that many industries wanted them.

And Blackburn Manufacturing has exploited its competitive advantage in the marking flag market to the fullest. When you see small plastic flags used at construction sites, in landscaping projects and nurseries, or by utilities, chances are Blackburn Manufacturing made those flags. Without leaving the niche it dominates, the company has added accessory products, such as tape, marking paint, and different types of staffs on which to hang the flags.

"We have always been a very self-sufficient company in that we build our own flag machines from scratch and our own buildings as they have become necessary for expansion," says Jim.

The 57-employee company, now based in Neligh, Nebraska, has also remained a family operation. Jim's brother, Bob, manages one of two factories. His brother-in-law is sales manager. Also, Jim's daughter and Bob's son are both active in the business.

Just because Blackburn Manufacturing was first, doesn't mean it can depend on maintaining its leadership without effort. The company keeps profit margins low enough to discourage big companies from trying to compete. Plain four-inch by five-inch flags sell for less than four cents apiece in orders of more than 25,000.

Obviously, volume is an important factor in Blackburn Manufacturing's success. The company sells 168 million marking flags each year and boasts 25,000 customers worldwide.

"I keep looking over my shoulder expecting someone to invent a better mouse trap, make a better flag," Jim says. "But it's such a niche product, and we have always been very customer-oriented."

# 21. PAY ATTENTION TO YOU

### Don't let the hard work of starting and building a business destroy your health.

■ ■ ■

**W**hen Ann Reizer and Marshall Hovivian started Martin Integrated Systems in Orange, California, in 1989, energy and good health were their most abundant assets, although they appeared nowhere on the balance sheet.

The pair had worked together at a general contracting company and decided to create their own specialty subcontracting firm to install ceilings in commercial buildings. Marshall had the business contacts and construction expertise. Ann, who holds an MBA and is a certified public accountant, handled the job estimating and the books.

Instead of aiming to be the low bidder, Martin Integrated emphasized high quality and service. That was a unique philosophy in the construction industry, Ann says. It required plenty of hands-on work in setting up the management systems and training workers to follow the high-service style.

"We had to be there to put our imprint on every procedure, every job," she says. "We were feeling our way along. When a client called up and said, 'I need it tomorrow,' we had to be able to say yes."

They worked 14-hour days, six days a week.

Most of her life Ann had two colds a year, one each spring and fall, with rare bouts of the flu or bronchitis thrown in. Once she became a business-owner she worked through minor illnesses. If she got tired, she drank a Coke.

"I'm one of those people who thinks sleeping is a waste of time," Ann says. "But you only have so much reserve you can draw on," she warns. "Then every cold turns into bronchitis; every bronchitis turns into asthma."

In 1995, Ann had a stroke.

In hindsight, warning signs were plentiful. She had been in two car accidents, so she didn't sleep well because of continual pain. A personal relationship ended. Those factors wore down her immune system, Ann says, and she got bronchitis that antibiotics couldn't stop. She had four asthma attacks that sent her to the emergency room. Twice she was hospitalized.

"I basically ignored all of it," Ann says.

She believes her unrelenting work schedule combined with poor diet and little exercise contributed to her deteriorating health, which culminated in the stroke. How else could she explain it? She has low cholesterol and no evidence of heart problems.

Now Ann has occasional seizures. The damage to her lungs is permanent. Ann used to go on vacations where she hiked eight miles without breathing hard. Now she can't walk on a treadmill without taking a breathing treatment first. Fatigue is a constant companion. After three hours of activity, she needs a nap.

Ann says she and Marshall should have trained others so the company wasn't so dependent on their constant presence. After the management and financial systems were in place, they could have done that, but they didn't change gears.

Marshall was able to keep Martin Integrated going after Ann's stroke by working even harder. His wife, Cindy, a company officer, also put in long hours, and the rest of the staff scrambled to learn and take on the work Ann had done.

Fortunately for Ann, Martin Integrated had bought disability insurance for the two partners just a year before her stroke. It replaces her salary, so she doesn't have financial worries along with the nagging health concerns.

"Most start-ups don't buy disability insurance because it's tremendously expensive, especially for women," Ann says.

Will she ever be able to work full time again?

"I can dream," she laughs.

"Would I have escaped all the health problems if I had taken better care of myself? It's too iffy to say," Ann theorizes. "But definitively I *can* say that if you work 14, 18 hours a day long enough, you will ruin your health."

# 22. RIGHT FORM

Consider all the consequences of the legal
structure you choose for your business.

■ ■ ■

When Alliance Systems spun off from Honeywell, Inc., it had to create all the support systems formerly drawn from the parent company. Employee James Doyle convinced his management that it ought to outsource the information systems department.

"We learned on the job how to find the right contractors," he says. "But we literally worked ourselves out of a job."

Jim was forced to retire at the age of 64. He wasn't ready for the rocking chair, so in 1994 he started DM & Associates, a Plymouth, Minnesota, consulting firm, to help companies find and contract with outside companies to manage their information services. He later brought in his former boss.

The legal structure an owner chooses can make a big difference in taxes and liability. The most common form of ownership is the sole proprietorship. But an owner may choose to form a partnership, an S corporation, a regular or C corporation, or the newest option, a limited liability company.

Jim opted for the limited liability company (LLC), but soon discovered it was a costly mistake, given his tax situation.

The LLC has some advantages for certain companies. It combines tax aspects of a partnership with the limited liability of a corporation. Many accounting firms have switched from partnerships to LLCs. While some states impose a business income tax on LLCs, the federal government and most states tax only the incomes of individual LLC members.

An S corporation passes income to individuals, at which point it is taxed as individual income, like it is under an LLC. However, the income is considered a disbursement or dividend, which, in Jim's case, is better for his retirement status.

Incorporation is a more costly and cumbersome choice of ownership because of fees and paperwork requirements. Small businesses that incorporate usually choose S corporation status because income is taxed just once. In a C corporation, income is taxed twice: as the corporation's income and a second time as its shareholders' individual incomes. Certain types of companies that have more than 75 shareholders or want to give some owners preferred stock must incorporate as C corporations.

It would have been simpler for Jim to set up a sole proprietorship or partnership, but many consulting firms these days want the limited liability that LLCs and corporations offer.

The sole proprietorship is the simplest and least expensive way to start a business. If a company loses money in the early years, these losses can shelter other income. However, the owner is on the hook for all financial and professional liabilities of the business. If the company's assets don't cover its debts, creditors can go after the owner's personal assets.

Partnerships involve more than one person and expose every partner to personal liability for the company's debts.

Weighing the pluses and minuses of the various forms of business ownership, Jim cancelled the LLC in 1998, and DM & Associates became an S corporation.

As DM & Associates' major corporate clients struggle to find employees with information systems expertise at affordable salaries, the company finds plenty of work both on its own and as a subcontractor to general-purpose management consulting firms.

A booming economy and fast-changing technology created a shortage of qualified experts to manage the expanding communication and computer services of every company that needs them, Jim says. "It's a matter of management control, resources, and costs," he continues. "It's cheaper for an outside company to house the necessary computers and hire experts and spread the cost over a lot of companies instead of every company trying to maintain its own."

# 23. YOU DON'T HAVE TO HAVE ALL THE ANSWERS

### It is acceptable to ask questions. It's not a sign that you're incompetent or lacking in professionalism.

■ ■ ■

**S**ometimes a layoff can be the prod needed to launch a new business. It was for Jennifer Jackson-Smith, who lost her job as a software engineer in 1991.

"I was devastated by the layoff and never wanted that to happen again, so I was determined to start my own business and do something I liked," Jennifer says.

For years, she had loved planning events for her church and other nonprofit groups. Her only pay was the experience and enjoyment. To turn that activity into a paying business, Jennifer used her severance pay to complete a college certificate program in meeting planning. She then launched Meeting Details Unlimited in Pasadena, California, in 1992. The company plans trade shows and special events around the country.

However, she was afraid to ask questions of both other business owners and her own clients.

"I associated asking for help with showing that I didn't know everything," Jennifer says. "It must have been some latent fear of appearing less than a superwoman."

Many new business owners share Jennifer's fear. It usually doesn't stem from arrogance, but from insecurity. Who would give a big contract to a business owner who doesn't know what she's doing?

Even though Jennifer had degrees in math and computer science, her lack of an MBA and a background in business made her feel insecure. She believed she had to portray an image of the expert to clients and other entrepreneurs at business gatherings.

"I had always been the independent type," she says. "In the engineering field, it is usually a solo effort until it is time to integrate the product. So realizing that I do need others and learning how to ask for help has been my biggest challenge."

Not asking questions stunted the growth of Meeting Details Unlimited, Jennifer says.

She attended networking and professional meetings that should have brought her new business, but yielded nothing. The contracts she did earn were less profitable and more troublesome than they should have been because of the lack of communication between Jennifer and the client. She didn't get the support and effort from clients that she expected, and, she admits, they probably felt the same way about her.

"I looked at my tax returns and realized I didn't make any money. I tracked my hours and discovered I was working for minimum wage," she says. "That's when you know something's not right."

Determined to take Meeting Details Unlimited to the next level in business, Jennifer bridled her insecurity and started asking questions.

"With clients, I don't take anything for granted. I ask the most basic questions, and if they think I'm not qualified, that's up to them. I want to know the answers," Jennifer says. Her early experiences showed her the types of misunderstandings likely to arise, so she carefully wrote them into contracts.

"Do not let the client back you into a corner and make you feel like your best is not good enough or that you are less than a professional," Jennifer advises. "Even if you don't have all of the answers, realize it's O.K. to ask questions."

Jennifer also turned to other business experts for guidance. Such conversations not only provide valuable information; they give the business owner benchmarks to guide pricing, levels of service, and value-added activities that enhance a company's reputation. Ask questions and you soon discover that others have dealt with issues you thought were unique to your company.

"Now I meet and ask for the help of people who are more experienced in areas that I am not, such as marketing," she says. "It still feels uncomfortable. However, the thought of not attaining my goals and dreams is even more uncomfortable."

# 24.

## MARGIN OF SUCCESS

Concentrate on specialty products
with the highest profit margins.

■ ■ ■

**D**ennis Tursso lost his position as regional sales manager for a large label maker when the company was sold. That experience convinced him that the only way he could control his destiny was to own his own business. Therefore, in 1968, he bought a bankrupt printing company for $10,000.

"It didn't matter what kind of company I owned; creativity knows no bounds," Dennis says.

Initially, the company was just another sheet printer doing jobs that every other printer was doing. Survival would be a struggle; large profits, nearly impossible.

"If you have a commodity product, the only way to be a winner is to be so large that you can sell in enormous quantity," Dennis says. "If you're small, you have to have something new that saves time and money and that no one else is doing."

It was clear to Dennis that specialty products had higher profit margins that would enhance the value of every aspect of Tursso Companies in St. Paul, Minnesota. To find a few products in which to specialize, he worked long and hard to understand what his customers wanted. Dennis eventually chose pharmaceutical labels, envelopes for professional photo processing labs, appointment books for hairdressers, and labels applied in the mold to plastic containers like shampoo bottles.

To dominate these fields, Tursso Companies had to do more than print labels. It had to develop equipment and processes that it could patent. Then the company would make money whether printing the labels itself or licensing the rights to other printers. One of its patents eliminates problematic static electricity from the in-mold labeling process. It holds another patent for accordion-like labels that can be attached permanently to medicine bottles.

Just getting approval from the U.S. Food and Drug Administration (FDA) to print pharmaceutical labels required Tursso Companies to pass a stringent audit. As Dennis became an expert in that industry, he realized that the FDA eventually would require drug companies to put all usage information on the container.

"People throw away the information sheets, then they forget what the doctor told them," Dennis says. "That becomes a problem with older people who take several medicines. But there's a lot of information, and those medicine vials are so small."

Tursso Companies' solution is a multifolded sheet that can be resealed many times. The company holds worldwide patents on that label, and its sales potential is huge. Even before the company started marketing the label, a customer placed a $30,000 order.

The winnowing process must be continual in order for a company to concentrate only on specialty products with the highest profit margins. Tursso Companies completely reorganized in 1997 to set the stage for future growth. It sold its legal form printing division and probably will sell the appointment book division. Those actions were necessary for the company to concentrate on obtaining its ISO 9002 certification. (International Organization for Standardization in Geneva establishes a procedure by which a company can document the quality of its design, production, inspection, and testing. A company must achieve ISO certification before it can do business in a growing number of countries.)

"I didn't really want to grow the company, [but] my employees wanted to grow," Dennis says. "And if you want to grow, sometimes you have to reshape the company."

Dennis is positioning the company for success far into the future, even after he is no longer involved. That's rare. Entrepreneurs and their companies often are inseparable. As Dennis explains it, "My company is very much a part of me. The heartache, setbacks, problems all flow through my body."

# 25. KNOW YOUR STRENGTHS

Evaluate your strengths to emphasize
your business's most lucrative
aspects from the beginning.

■ ■ ■

After 12 years as a corporate secretary at a major aerospace company, Jo Ann Fischer saw the industry shrinking after the end of the Cold War. Therefore, in the early 1990s, she volunteered to be laid off with a severance package to finance her long-time dream of opening her own business. In March 1993, Jo Ann started Write When U Need It, a secretarial service, in her Fullerton, California, home.

"Timing is everything," Jo Ann says. "My kids were raised. My husband had a great job. And I always wanted to do my own thing."

Jo Ann offered every possible typing, writing, and graphic design aid available from independent business support services. In addition to the writing and computer software skills she had honed at her previous employment, Jo Ann used her Macintosh computer to create flyers and brochures.

"Brochures were fun, almost like playing," she says. "However, I soon discovered that not only did clients not realize how time intensive this kind of artwork was, they tended to complain about the costs involved."

In addition to the hassle, the brochure work tended to be one-time projects that did not lead to continuing business relationships. This was no way to build a company. Soon Jo Ann realized that not only was the writing easier and more enjoyable for her, but clients appreciated it more.

"I discovered that people, in general, are extremely grateful to find someone who can write an error-free page, letter, contract, or proposal for them," she says. "I should have had the guts to focus on what I loved most from day one."

Out of fear they won't get enough work, many service entrepreneurs don't narrow their offerings when they first open. They often take on projects though they have little knowledge or experience in the area; therefore, they spend hours getting up to speed instead of earning money. Over time, they discover, as Jo Ann did, that they can do a better job for their clients—and, therefore, be more profitable—if they emphasize the specific skills they enjoy most and are in greatest demand.

In Jo Ann's case, she spent seven months taking small-business classes and reading everything about self-employment she could get her hands on. However, it wasn't until after she had been in business a while that she did an in-depth study of her own strengths in the secretarial service industry. Eventually, Jo Ann worked up the courage to refocus her business to emphasize newsletter creation, proofreading, business writing, and editing.

"I do a lot of proofreading. Consultants fax me their proposals, even letters. I can proofread it faster and better [than they can], so it's a more productive use of time for both of us," she says.

Jo Ann completely stopped doing spreadsheets, databases, and straight typing. She refers those jobs to other secretarial services that specialize in them. If a client wants Jo Ann to do graphics as part of a larger project, such as a newsletter, she charges more for it.

This shift in focus has enabled her to develop long-term, more profitable relationships with her clients and give better quality work for less effort.

"I'm much happier now," Jo Ann says. "It has taken a lot of pieces—hard work, learning, laughter, frustration—to get where I am today."

# 26.  DON'T TAKE IT PERSONALLY

In business, rejection isn't personal. Make
enough calls, and eventually you will get jobs.

■ ■ ■

Leticia Herrera got into the cleaning business to keep a promise to a friend. The friend had done her a favor and in return asked for the name of a Hispanic-owned janitorial service. Leticia's referral backed out of the job at the last minute, so she recruited her mother and aunt—the best cleaners she knew—and did the job herself.

"I never even cleaned my own house," she says. "I didn't think of getting paid; I just had to keep my word."

When the check arrived a month later, Leticia couldn't even remember what she had called her "company." But she realized that the $1,200 payment minus her expenses was more than she made in two weeks at her regular job.

So Extra Clean, Inc. (ECI), became an official business in Chicago, Illinois, in 1989. Its seemingly easy beginning quickly gave way to the harsh realities of trying to win cleaning contracts without a corporate history, reputation, or savings account.

Perseverance was Leticia's only nourishment in a steady diet of rejection by potential customers. It toughened her skin and her resolve.

"In small business, we get too personal. My business is my baby. That's me. That's my reputation," Leticia says. "But it's not personal."

Customers are looking for solutions for themselves. They are not trying to harm or help fledgling companies. To win business, entrepreneurs need to offer those solutions. And they need to offer as many times as it takes to find a yes.

Leticia learned that if she made enough sales calls, eventually someone would throw a little work her way. Sometimes it took a hundred calls. Then she learned that if she did a good job, more work would follow.

"When I first started, I did anything," she says. "They never give you the easy stuff. They give you whatever no one else could do, expecting you to fail like everyone else."

Her willingness to tackle the most difficult cleaning tasks led ECI to a lucrative niche that has become the main focus of the company: stone cleaning and restoration.

During the early 1990s, the janitorial industry was changing. Small companies like ECI had increasing difficulty competing with large corporations for routine maintenance contracts. ECI almost went bankrupt.

Leticia asked one client for additional work, and he said other cleaning companies had been unable to clean the terrazzo in his building. Leticia didn't know how to clean it either, but she loved art and architecture, so she turned to European experts to learn how to clean marble and other stone.

"We were like bulldogs," she says. "Four or five other companies had failed. I wasn't about to."

Success on that project led to other unusual and emergency cleaning projects. That's when Leticia decided to ease out of routine maintenance to concentrate on stone cleaning and restoration, which have higher profit margins. The new focus has led to projects for Carrara Marble & Mosaic Co., the Chicago Museum of Contemporary Art, the Democratic National Convention, the Field Museum, and hundreds more needing the specialty cleaning and restoration service.

Cleaning and restoring stone and metal is labor intensive, so most of ECI's competitors don't want to do it. "I use European products, but in Italy, they take a year to clean something. Can you imagine me taking a year for one of my clients?" says Leticia, who loves the specialty's artistic nature.

Leticia's persistence in seeking contracts has grown ECI to 90 employees and more than $2 million. "Success is a daily thing," she says. "Even if I have bad days, I will succeed if I don't give up. Every failure I have had has been followed by a greater blessing."

# 27.

# THE VALUE OF
# A CALM CENTER

You must cultivate the wisdom to know what
you can and cannot change. This attitude
will help you remain calm in decision making
and stand by that which you believe.

■  ■  ■

**W**hen Isabel and Gary Hendricks moved to Bend, Oregon, in 1969, they had two choices: start their own business or starve. There has always been an electrician in Isabel's family, including her husband, so the pair started Hendricks' Electric, a housing and commercial electrical contractor.

"It was a real mom and pop operation," Isabel says.

In 1982, Isabel had the opportunity to go in a different direction installing traffic signals and highway and airport runway lights. She and several partners opened H & H Electric in Portland, Oregon. Three years later, she bought them out. Although her husband later became a consultant and supervisor for the company, H & H has always been Isabel's domain.

What Isabel learned almost immediately was that heavy electrical contracting is a man's world.

"I either could have butted heads all the time or made the situation work for me," she says. "I learned to learn from men and work with them. It takes a long time to learn what works and earn their respect."

Isabel came from a black-and-white world. If she went to the store with a dollar in her pocket and a loaf of bread was $1.05, she couldn't buy it.

"Men don't think that way," she says. "They always deal in grays, in politics. You scratch my back, and I'll scratch yours."

When she removed the emotion and viewed such arrangements dispassionately, Isabel had to admit she found nothing wrong with many business relationships. But others did not match her own ethics.

"I won't chop someone's price out of my bids or make trouble for someone else," she says.

Isabel keeps a line of credit for working capital, but no long-term debt. She owns her own equipment and building. She has had the same bonding company, accountant, and bank for 15 years.

There may be many aspects of her industry that Isabel cannot change, but the work environment at H & H isn't one of them.

"I've had jobs where I have gotten up on mornings and I bawled because I didn't want to go to work," she says. "I don't want my employees to feel like that."

When H & H had a highway lighting project during its first year, Isabel worked as a laborer alongside her men.

"It's very important to show, in a sincere way, what I think of my workers," she says. "I believe in rewarding on merit."

H & H is a nonunion shop, and Isabel has had her run-ins with the unions over the years.

"The unions have cost me a fortune, but I keep my anger in tow and continue to do what's right," she says. "I remember what my mom used to say: If you give them enough rope, they'll hang themselves. You don't have to do anything underhanded."

Isabel has 25 employees, many of whom have been with her since H & H started. She pays better wages and benefits than the union scale. The company has a profit-sharing program that employees decide where to invest.

When a female employee had a baby, Isabel allowed her to bring the infant to work and set up a crib and swing in the office.

"You can't imagine what that baby did for morale around here," Isabel says. "My big ol' tough guys were so gentle with her."

# 28. BAD VIBES

Check out your location and building carefully.
You can't imagine the damage to your
company if the building is poorly
maintained or half-empty.

■ ■ ■

When Sharon Kelly started a company to publish how-to books for the spa industry, she couldn't find an office in downtown Anchorage, Alaska, in which she could share secretarial and office services. Therefore, she decided to open her own executive office suite. She looked for space for more than four years. Office building owners wanted three years' rent in advance to take a chance on both an unproven concept and someone who had no experience in the endeavor. Finally, she was able to rent 3,000 square feet in an empty office building, and in 1992 Sharon opened Midtown Executive Office Suite.

"An empty building is a difficult location for a start-up business," she now says. "Couple this with a building that isn't kept clean, and it's devastating. If you're on the second floor, as I was, you have no control over the first impression people have of your business.

"Even if your suite is high class and the staff extremely competent, clients still judge you by the mess outside the door," she says.

Location and appearance are important to many types of businesses. Sharon recommends that new entrepreneurs visit a site they're thinking about leasing at different times of day both on weekdays and on the weekend. If she had visited the office building at night, she would have noticed that it had no outside signs or lights. It was virtually invisible. Sharon also recommends talking to the building's janitors and tenants to learn how well a building and its grounds are maintained.

Other factors can be important in evaluating commercial space. A company might want street-level access, ample free parking, or nearby restaurants, for example. It was important to Sharon to have her executive suite in a top-quality office building.

She avoided moving out of the old location for several years because she had invested her life savings, $30,000, in tenant improvements in the suite. However, when she lost her last client in December 1996, she started looking elsewhere.

In October 1997, Sharon moved Midtown Executive Office Suite to another building. Because she now had a track record in the executive suite industry, Sharon was able to persuade another landlord to accept her business. However, she now applied the lessons she learned from her first office search. She talked with the cleaning service and tenants, who told her the new space was immaculately maintained and any problems were repaired promptly. She negotiated an outside sign for her company. She visited at night to make sure passersby could see the building. She also insisted on a clause that no interior construction for tenant build-outs would disrupt her business during working hours. Sharon recommends that entrepreneurs check a building owner's background for lawsuits or unpaid taxes. "This one entity can make or break your business," she says. "Make sure it is in tune with you and your company."

Each location has a personality that affects your business. In her former location, Sharon received secretarial work from some tenants, but the new building houses larger tenants that have their own secretaries. However, the new location is across the street from a business hotel, whose residents bring her much more walk-in business than she used to have. In both locations, her executive suites have attracted traveling salespeople, large corporations looking for branch offices, and home-based entrepreneurs in need of commercial addresses and meeting space.

Midtown Executive Office Suite is no longer alone in town. Two other executive suites have opened, but Sharon doesn't consider them competition. One is a low-priced walk-in; the other has a large advertising budget.

"I see them as allies," she says. "If they're full, they refer people to me, and if my suite isn't right for [a prospective tenant], I refer him to one of the other executive suites."

# 29. STRIKE A BALANCE

Although businesses should specialize, they need enough diversity to avoid economic downturns that hit one industry or region.

■ ■ ■

The entrepreneurial bug bit Terry Anderson after he had worked for others as a design engineer, buyer, and salesperson for the better part of the 1960s and 1970s. He and his wife, Nancy, started Omni Tech, a manufacturer's representative firm, in their Pewaukee, Wisconsin, home in 1978. The firm sold fabricated metal products. It grew rapidly to $7.5 million in sales, with 80 percent of the business coming from the agriculture and heavy equipment industries.

In 1981 and 1982, both industries hit a recession. Omni Tech's business declined 70 percent in 18 months. A $4 million contract with Caterpillar Tractor plummeted to $50,000, and a $1.5 million contract with International Harvester plunged to $75,000.

"I wasn't street savvy about running a business," Terry says. If he had been, he would have avoided concentrating too much on two major accounts with just one type of product.

To survive in business, Terry reduced the company back to its core and returned to making his own sales calls again. But for long-term success, Terry decided on a different strategy.

"It was imperative that Omni Tech never again put all its eggs in one basket, but have several separate businesses," he says. "If one business cycle was down, another part would be up."

The key was to diversify while still specializing, a neat trick that many entrepreneurs can't pull off in a crisis mode. To his credit, Terry didn't give in to the temptation to try to sell all products to everyone. Instead, he developed two parallel specialty divisions that matched his engineering and sales background.

One part of the business would design and make specialized sheet metal products for organizations that lacked in-house capabilities to build their own. Drawing on his engineering background, Terry designed and patented an enclosure for Apple IIe computers for the Milwaukee, Wisconsin, public schools. The fixtures eliminated tampering and secured the computers to desktops to avoid theft. Soon Omni Tech was selling these units to schools throughout the country.

A short time later, to complete Terry's diversified specialty strategy, Omni Tech started building custom IBM-compatible computers for customers' specific needs.

The diversified specialty strategy was a wise one, Terry says.

When the price of Apple IIe computers declined from $2,100 to $600, schools no longer felt the need to protect the equipment with costly security enclosures. Instead of suffering another financial tailspin, Omni Tech expanded its computer division while its design technology division developed other products.

The designers came up with a modular, wall-mounted enclosure for computers at 2,200 Kentucky Fried Chicken fast-food restaurants. Later they created computer shelves for the back offices in 7-Eleven convenience stores owned by Southland Corp.

For its part, the computer division doesn't try to sell to the mass market, Terry says. "We sell personal computers to a targeted list of large corporations that we invite to become customers of ours in a win-win situation."

Omni Tech's sales grew from $1.2 million in 1989 to $105 million eight years later. The company moved into an 18,000-square-foot building in 1993 and added an 11,000-square-foot office in 1995.

Because of the product mix, Omni Tech doesn't have a problem financing its growth. One side is capital intensive with high inventory and receivables, while the other requires little up-front capital. However, the growth didn't proceed as smoothly as it sounds.

"It took us ten years to find the right path," Terry says, "but I didn't know what I didn't know."

# 30. INVESTMENTS THAT DIFFERENTIATE

Immediate investment in technology can set a
company apart and make it more difficult
for competitors to enter the market.

■ ■ ■

In 1984, Cameron James and Ken Mills were coworkers at an Ohio video production company when they asked each other a simple question: Was corporate demand for video likely to grow in Columbus, Ohio? Of course. So the pair invested several thousand dollars to form Mills/James Productions. They rented the essential equipment and started making corporate videos for local businesses. Cameron and Ken worked as independent producers, contracting for the services needed on each project.

Mills/James rented the equipment it needed because, at that time, a broadcast-quality editing suite cost $2 million. That approach put Mills/James at the mercy of the companies that owned the equipment. Equipment availability limited the projects the company could go after. The obvious problem for startups is obtaining the cash to acquire the technology. Loans are difficult to come by. Investors want higher profit margins than many industries command. The entrepreneurs must take a gamble to buy barriers to their competition. Cameron admits he wasn't much of a risk taker. Surprised? Don't be. Many people who start businesses and grow them into major successes don't consider themselves speculators, just seizers of opportunity.

In 1988, Mills/James was given the opportunity to manage the video production division for Discovery Systems. Mills/James not only shared the profits, but gained access to $2 million in equipment. The company added postproduction and graphics services to its offerings. Its staff more than doubled.

"That catapulted us to great growth and rapid expansion," Cameron says.

Mills/James derives a double benefit from owning the high-tech equipment required in its industry, he adds. Potential competitors have to spend more money to enter the market. And possessing equipment that few others have allows Mills/James to charge more for its services.

"In hindsight, I would have invested in technology immediately, although it would have required greater risk and careful planning," Cameron says.

Once Mills/James started reaping the benefits of owning its technology, it continued to make the investments that separated it from the competition. In 1990, the company built its own 25,000-square-foot production facility rather than convert an existing building, which is the more common approach. Five years later, the company added 22,000 square feet of space. Few production facilities offer the range of film, videoconferencing, special events, radio, television, CD-ROM, and Internet services that Mills/James has under one roof, Cameron says. The company's clients range from corporations to government agencies. Instead of being the tenant, the company rents its equipment and production facilities to advertising agencies and others.

In 1997, Mills/James was the 16th largest contract production company in the United States, with 130 employees and annual revenue of $15 million.

While Ohio isn't recognized as the heartland of the video industry, it has had a great influence on Mills/James' development into a one-stop source for media and special events, Cameron says.

"We have a fraction of the overhead in Columbus versus the West Coast or New York," he explains. "There are more boutique [limited-service] companies on the two coasts."

However, the Internet is changing the level of competition in the industry. Now a video company can put libraries of clients' videos on the Internet, and executives can view them on personal computers at their desks anywhere in the world. That opens new markets to Mills/James, but also opens its market strongholds to international companies.

"We work in a business that is changing at the speed of light," Cameron says. "It is change brought about by changing marketplaces, changing technologies, and changing customer demands. We must constantly reevaluate how we do things. What was good enough yesterday might not be good enough tomorrow.

"Change is not always easy, but it is essential. If you're not hurting, you're probably not growing."

# *31.* THE RIGHT STUFF

Obtain the right equipment in the beginning,
even if it costs more, because you will
spend more to buy it later.

■ ■ ■

In 1977, the Alaska Transportation Agency awarded Taquan Air Service, Inc., a permit to operate an air taxi service between Annette Island and Ketchikan International Airport in southeast Alaska. Owner Jerry Scudero's market research indicated that he could get plenty of business transporting loggers, tourists, and state Fish and Game Department employees. Still, he balked at the $80,000 price of a seven-seat deHavilland Beaver airplane. Instead, he settled for a $40,000, four-seat Cessna 180.

The smaller aircraft limited the amount of work Taquan Air could accept. In addition, the wear and tear on the Cessna 180, trying to do too much with too little, cost the company a great deal of money for maintenance and repair.

"I would have done a lot better more quickly if I had bought the larger plane," says Jerry, who was the company's only pilot in the early years. "I had so much freight in addition to people that I really loaded that 180 down. If I had bought a plane with more seats, I would have had more to sell."

Taquan Air couldn't keep up with the business so, in 1980, the company bought a Cessna 185 and a year later added a deHavilland Beaver.

"If you think the business is out there, make the financial commitment to the right equipment in the beginning because eventually you'll need it," Jerry advises.

During the mid-1980s, deregulation of the air charter industry brought enormous competition to Taquan Air's territory. While competitors slashed their prices, Taquan refused. It survived by strictly controlling costs and service area and maintaining high-quality service. Still, Jerry had learned his lesson about buying the needed equipment and facilities. He added four more aircraft by 1989.

His strategy paid off. The company doubled its sales in 1986 and 1987 and upped them by 25 percent in 1988. By 1989, Taquan Air was the second largest air taxi service in Alaska, with seven aircraft, 45 employees, and $2.1 million in sales. Jerry also added land and maintenance facilities along the Ketchikan waterfront for his float planes.

When the major competition closed its fixed-wing division in 1991, Taquan Air was prepared. The U.S. Forest Service awarded Taquan Air the contract to supply its fixed-wing air service in the Ketchikan region. The company doubled in size by the end of 1992.

Investing in the right equipment and facilities made that growth possible, Jerry says.

Now Jerry is taking his flight service in southeast Alaska in a new direction. In 1997, he sold some of his shares in Taquan Air to buy most of the assets of Ketchikan Air, including hangers and leases at Ketchikan International Airport. Again, the purchase of the right equipment and facilities made it possible for Jerry to start a commuter airline to serve southeast Alaska. The air taxi service and commuter airline have a total of 40 airplanes.

"It doesn't matter what business you're in, you have to get the right equipment to do the job," Jerry says. "You think 'I'm just a start-up. I have financial restraints.' But I know if I would have pressed it, I could have done something to obtain the bigger airplane [in the beginning].

"While we were able to get past the initial years," he says, "we could have progressed faster."

# *32.*  ONE SIZE DOESN'T
         FIT ALL

A product business requires different
management techniques and takes longer to
develop than a service business.

■ ■ ■

Elaine Floyd earned an engineering degree, but found that she had a natural talent for sales. When she started writing a newsletter for her clients, her employer soon asked her to prepare the company newsletter.

"They farmed out the layout to an advertising agency, and when I saw the bill, I said 'I'll do it for that amount,'" Elaine remembers.

She bought a Macintosh computer and an early version of Pagemaker software and started writing newsletters for other companies as well as her employer. In 1985, Elaine quit to produce newsletters full time.

"Who planned? I was about 24 at the time and just hanging on for the ride," she says.

Elaine was great at persuading others to hire her to produce their newsletters. She closed 90 percent of her sales, and soon she was grossing $250,000 and had five employees. But producing the newsletters was a hassle.

Service providers do a lot of handholding, client education, and face-to-face meetings. Each project is unique and can be sold only once. How much better, Elaine thought, to have one product that she could sell many times.

"I was doing public speaking to market my newsletter business, and I might get five potential clients and still have to do a lot of work to close the deal," she says. "If I had product, I could give one speech, get lots of sales, and have no follow-up."

At the same time, she married a college researcher whose career was likely to move them around the country. It was a good time to reinvent her business. Elaine came up with Newsletter Resources, a company that would sell both services and products—books—and operate wherever she lived. The company has moved to several states and currently is located in St. Louis, Missouri.

When Elaine wrote *Marketing with Newsletters* to teach how to design, write, and sell newsletters, she discovered that product and service businesses are managed differently. If she ran the product side of her business like she ran the services, she'd be out of business real quick.

While her newsletter services had expanded almost effortlessly, product sales take much longer to build and require knowledge of finances and inventory control, Elaine says. Product sales have a longer start-up curve. It is helpful to separate the two divisions if you want to do both within your company, she advises.

"A service gives you cash, but a product gives you P.I.G.: passive income generator," she says. "With a product, you don't have to give the same amount of effort to each account every day. But my book sales are more seasonal. I don't sell many in the summer."

Elaine's books require press releases, marketing to reviewers, and booksellers—things her services don't need. She developed a Web site to promote her books, seminars, and consulting. She had to add to her product line—in other words, write more books. Therefore, she wrote *Advertising from the Desktop, The Newsletter Editor's Desk Book, Making Money Writing Newsletters, Quick and Easy Newsletters, How to Create a Family Newsletter* and *Marketing Your Bookstore with a Newsletter. How to Market with Newsletters* is in its fourth edition.

"I had quick success with a service business, but you don't learn reality when that happens," Elaine says. "You can't necessarily repeat a quick success because you don't know how much of it was circumstantial and how much was skill.

"You always pay the price of admission into business success. Either you pay up front or sometime in the midlife of your company."

# 33. CHANGE TRANSFORMS

Anticipate how technology and other
economic and societal changes will
transform your business.

■ ■ ■

**W**anda Gozdz was a librarian who observed libraries' need for specialized resources in their legal and tax collections. When she started a service in 1979 to find reputable vendors to supply this authoritative material, their products all came on paper.

"Most attorneys have a huge attachment to paper; a lot of people do," Wanda says. "When I started, I thought I was going to have books forever."

That belief proved to be shortsighted in the technology revolution that followed. If Wanda hadn't changed her business philosophy to adapt to the new technology, her company, W. Gozdz Enterprises, Inc., in Plantation, Florida, would be just another relic in the museum of obsolete businesses.

Wanda's dilemma is not unusual. Tastes change. New materials hit the market. More efficient procedures replace "the way we've always done it."

Imagine the dumps filled with leisure suits, Edsel cars, and eight-track tape players. Cameras are now made of plastic. Baseball bats are aluminum and titanium, except in the major leagues. Toothpaste contains not only fluoride, but peroxide, baking soda, plaque and tartar fighters, and fake mint.

The federal government now posts its upcoming contract needs on the Internet and expects to receive contract proposals from companies of all sizes the same way. Many manufacturers demand that their suppliers comply with standardized quality procedures. Major retailers require their vendors to be tied to computers for automatic reordering of goods.

The savvy business owners—the survivors—must change, too.

W. Gozdz Enterprises was being pressured from both the supply and demand sides. The number of information suppliers dwindled because of consolidations and mergers. Wanda had fewer choices of vendors. And the remaining companies dictated the formats in which they would supply information.

At the same time, her customers—the libraries—started asking for information products to be provided online and on CD-ROM. Attorneys now can tap into their library systems from the computers on their desks. Their searches can be performed at the press of a button instead of over mind-numbing hours of reading.

"[Technology] won't do away with books, but it does change the way information is available," Wanda says.

To keep up, she had to learn computers and multimedia applications. Her marketing had to change, too.

"Young attorneys accept information regardless of its medium of delivery, but older attorneys think information is authoritative only if it comes from books," she says. "They have to be persuaded to accept these new products."

Wanda's willingness to adapt has opened new markets for her 20-employee company. She now consults with libraries about their equipment needs. Wanda also was hired to advise in the rebuilding of a library destroyed in a flood because she had expertise both as a librarian and as a multimedia user. And her training on the Internet and in multimedia has enabled Wanda to diversify into developing sites for the World Wide Web.

When Wanda consults with libraries, "I can see the big picture in the way information is supplied and disseminated. I set up policies and procedures and then turn them over to a library's staff."

Wanda's adaptation required a flexible personality, of course, but she also had to remain current in the changing developments in her industry and in her customers' needs. Change rarely happens without warning. However, in order to receive such warning, business owners must read industry publications. They must attend professional meetings, trade shows, industry conventions, and seminars. They must talk with their customers and, in cases like Wanda's, their customers' customers.

# *34.*　SEIZE GROWTH OPPORTUNITIES

Some opportunities are best taken
in the early years.

■　■　■

John T. Kott had a job refinishing appliances when he hit on an idea. Why not apply the same concept to sinks, bathtubs, and countertops? It would be less expensive and easier than replacing these items. However, no one was refinishing porcelain and fiberglass in 1953, so John had to develop the technology himself.

That's when he started Kott Koatings, Inc. He and his son, John M. Kott, began franchising the concept in 1973 and selling international franchises in 1990.

"We should have expanded into franchising 20 years earlier to spread our system across the country and overseas," says John M. "The cost obviously would be less and the expansion much greater because there was less competition and fewer governmental restrictions and paperwork in the good old days."

Some fledgling entrepreneurs buy franchises to gain instant experience, brand names, and proven systems of management. Some existing entrepreneurs sell franchises of their business packages as a way to grow their companies. Kott Koatings, headquartered in Foothill Ranch, California, is a service franchise (instead of a product franchise like McDonald's), which was a concept virtually unknown in the 1950s when the company began. Even when the Kotts started contemplating the idea in the early 1970s, only a few service franchises, such as H&R Block tax preparation and Roto Rooter plumbing, existed.

"We went to a franchise attorney and said, 'Can this be done?' and he said, 'Sure, we can do anything,'" John M. says. "But it wasn't that easy."

The basic business of refinishing porcelain remained the same, but the Kotts had to revamp and modify their procedures to guide franchisees. To maintain quality, the company sells its bathtub glazes only through its franchisees.

"We have to train people to use our products because they depend on application technology," John M. says.

If Kott Koatings had figured out the franchising details in those early years, the company would have avoided fees and reporting regulations that most states now require.

California, where Kott Koatings is located, adopted the nation's first law governing franchise investments in 1970. The Uniform Franchise Offering Circular was developed originally by the Midwest Securities Commissioners Association in 1975 and is monitored now by the North American Securities Administrators Association. In 1989, the Federal Trade Commission chimed in with the first nationwide franchise disclosure regulation. Individual states have adapted the uniform circular, so national franchisers currently have dozens of modifications with which to comply.

These laws and regulations cropped up in response to investor complaints of abuses and deceptions by franchise sellers. It's not that the laws are unworthy, but they do complicate and add expense to the franchising process. Franchisers started avoiding some states, like Michigan, because their franchising rules and fees were so burdensome, John M. says. Even today, Kott Koatings has just one franchise in Michigan.

In the early 1970s, Kott Koatings received so many purchase requests from foreign entrepreneurs that it started exporting its service franchises. This move brought on an entirely new regulatory process.

The company's first effort was in Canada because the country is so similar to the United States, John M. says. "We went through as many rules and as much paperwork, but after you go through it once, it becomes routine."

The process was more complicated and costly in other countries. The U.S. Department of Commerce and consulates in various countries facilitated meetings in the countries, but negotiations took a long time, John T. says. Many foreign entrepreneurs had been burned by frauds with glossy brochures and nothing else to sell, so these potential buyers wanted to visit Kott's manufacturing plant to make sure the company was real. The Kotts endured this process and expense to achieve diversity.

"We went into a wide range of countries so if the economy is bad in one country or region, we still have strong sales in other regions," explains John M.

Kott has franchisees in more than 35 foreign countries and has won national awards for outstanding export performance. Nevertheless, the Kotts believe their reach would be more expansive with less investment if they had seized the franchising opportunity two decades earlier.

# 35. AFTER ALL THIS, WHAT?

Establish a retirement program in the
early years of business instead of waiting
for a more affluent period.

■ ■ ■

**W**orking in corporate America was a thankless grind for Gerard Moulin. For a decade after earning his engineering degree, Gerard worked for other engineering firms. His habit of working long hours eventually put him on a diet of heartburn medicine two or three times a day.

"I was always salaried, so I didn't make any more by working more hours," Gerard says. "I decided if I was going to work so hard, it might as well be for myself."

So in 1986, Gerard established Ohm Corporation in Orange, California, an electrical and mechanical engineering firm specializing in heavy industrial and commercial projects. The company also prepares engineering studies for insurance companies and attorneys.

Immediately, Gerard saved $60 a month, just on heartburn medicine.

Gerard's two regrets in his successful run are that he didn't start sooner. That is, start his own company. *And* start saving for his retirement. Retirement just isn't uppermost in an entrepreneur's mind at the beginning of a venture, Gerard acknowledges.

"But it should be," he says. "A friend tried to talk me into saving for retirement when I was in my 20s, but I said I didn't have any money.

"My plan was to retire at 50. I'm 48. It's not going to happen."

Setting aside even a small amount each month can make a huge difference in the long run. For example, if you start setting aside $100 a month when you're 35, by age 65 you will have $95,103 (based on a modest 8 percent annual return on investment). Wait until you're 45 to start, and you'll have $34,604 at retirement. Start at age 55, and you'll have a paltry $7,348—hardly enough to retire on.

Gerard finally started putting money into an individual retirement account in 1990. However, IRA tax-deductible contributions are limited to $2,000 a year, so Gerard soon established a self-employed pension (SEP)-IRA, the most common choice for the self-employed. The plan allowed him to contribute as much as 15 percent of his income, also tax deductible. SEP-IRAs also require employers to fund plans for all employees.

"I don't think you should shy away from giving employees a retirement plan," Gerard says. "It's cheaper than not giving yourself one."

Gerard could have chosen a 401(k) plan, but the regulations and reporting requirements are complex for small companies. He also could have chosen a Savings Incentive Match Plan for Employees (SIMPLE). However, with a SEP-IRA, he could vary the contribution amount each year. That can be important for companies whose revenues fluctuate.

Since Gerard established his SEP-IRA, the federal government approved a Roth IRA. Although the contributions to this plan aren't tax deductible, interest and future payouts are. Roth IRAs tend to be more suitable for people who have long investment times until retirement.

Investment advisers sometimes recommend using a combination of these plans, depending on each entrepreneur's financial and life circumstances.

Although he is unhappy he waited so long to begin saving for retirement, Gerard is satisfied with his plan. And he's applying the lesson he learned to the rest of his family. He has set up retirement savings plans for all three of his children and his toddler granddaughter.

"You need to have a long-term plan when you're young," Gerard says. "I know it's hard for a 20-year-old to think that way, but it's amazing how fast the years go by.

"Start a small plan and grow into it. You *are* your retirement."

**19.** When starting your venture, create a new support system of business colleagues, suppliers, and customers to replace your old corporate ties.

**20.** If you're not the first to come up with a business idea, sharpen it until it is your own.

**21.** Your business may be your life, but hobbies, vacations, and getaways lengthen that life.

**22.** Ask your accountant and attorney to explain all the legal and financial pros and cons of various ownership structures for your specific business.

**23.** Never assume; always ask.

**24.** Put your resources into your most profitable products and services. The revenues should follow profits, not the other way around.

**25.** Say no to projects that don't draw on your strengths or that customers will not pay top dollar for.

**26.** The world isn't out to sabotage your business. Put your energy into building your business, not feeling offended.

**27.** Both the system and long-time experts in your industry will work with you if you look for win-win proposals instead of ways to hurt others.

**28.** Trust is fine, but check every detail of your lease and negotiate out terms harmful to your company.

**29.** If your business's specialty teeters on too narrow a foundation, broaden it to give yourself better balance.

**30.** When buying equipment for your business, distinguish between the niceties and the true catapults that will launch you past your competition.

**31.** Buy the very best you can afford. It will save you money in the long run.

**32.** If you're adding products to your services, treat them like a separate business.

**33.** Study forecasts, futurists and trends. The world is changing much faster than you think.

**34.** That enticing opportunity you're waiting to take someday may not come according to your schedule. If your research says it makes sense, go for it.

**35.** Where will you be in 15 years? 30 years? Plan the path and save to get there.

# PART 3

# THE MONEY CHASE

**. . .**

**M**oney is the new business's most obvious need. Yet even in this arena, new owners have many lessons to learn. The most important is how hungry a young business is for resources and how your money never goes as far as you imagined when the baby was just a gleam in your eye.

To begin, you must develop a system that enables you to understand exactly where your company stands financially. Fortunately, many low-priced, easy-to-use accounting software programs can explain the money side of your business. They can help you control your costs and live within your means, even if you own a business with wild seasonal gyrations.

If you don't have enough personal resources, you have to turn to those who do. They won't be as eager to part with their money as you think they should. You may pay dearly for use of their money. You may even find that you have to give them control over your business in exchange for their money.

Although the loudest entrepreneurial complaint regards the scarcity of money sources, perhaps the most problematic issue is pricing. As with early decisions, described in Part 2, the new business owner often lacks the confidence and experience to set a price that customers will pay and will allow the owner to make a profit. Hint: most set their prices too low.

# *36.*  LEARN TO READ

To understand all the financial aspects of
your business, learn to read and interpret
balance sheets and income statements.

■  ■  ■

**A**nyone who loves to shop by mail probably knows the Lillian Vernon
Corp. catalogs. They bring thousands of household, gardening, kitchen,
Christmas and other gift items to the at-home buyer. More than 1,300 year-
round employees and thousands of seasonal workers send out $160 million
in merchandise annually.

It's hard to imagine that the whole thing started with a monogrammed
purse and belt sold through a sixth-of-a-page ad in *Seventeen* magazine in
1951. Lillian designed and made the purse and belt with the help of her
father, Herman Menasche, who owned a leather goods manufacturing plant
in New York.

Lillian was a 21-year-old pregnant housewife in need of more family
income. To help make ends meet, she invested $495 of the money she had
received as wedding gifts to buy the ad offering the purse for $2.99 and the
belt for $1.99. Three dollars and two dollars seemed too pricy to Lillian, but
$2.95 and $1.95 weren't profitable.

Lillian's total investment was $2,000. She hoped for a $1,000 profit.
Within the first three months, she received $32,000 in orders. And Lillian
Vernon was transformed from a housewife to an entrepreneur.

However, lack of financial know-how stymied Lillian's decision making in building her mail-order company. She didn't even own an adding
machine in those days, but a friendly banker let her use his once a week.

"Understanding the financial aspects is the one area where I had little
knowledge and experience in the 1950s," Lillian says. "Learning to read
balance sheets and income statements before I launched my business would
have helped."

These financial documents probably are foreign to someone who has
never owned a business and, unfortunately, to some who have. A balance
sheet details a company's assets (cash, inventory, equipment), liabilities
(accounts payable, loans) and capital (equity in the business). The bottom

line is the company's net worth. An income statement, often called a profit-and-loss statement, shows a company's financial performance over a period of time. This document breaks out every type of revenue and expense so the business owner can see trends. For example, if telephone charges are running higher than budgeted, the owner can investigate why and either take steps to control spending or adjust the budget to reflect the needed additional spending.

Even an entry-level college accounting class would have expanded Lillian's understanding of her accountant's calculations. Financial information helps the business owner develop a realistic budget, but its value is even more important in developing the vision for growth.

"[My accountant] could tell me what was selling, but I needed to translate that information into decisions regarding production, advertising, and future expansion of product lines," Lillian says.

She learned the financial side by trial and error and by hiring quality guidance through the formative years. Many of the early decisions Lillian made in her gut. With a gift for shopping, she added gold-plated pins and rings, a monogrammed bookmark that has remained one of the company's top sellers for more than four decades, and a brass door knocker for homes with just one bathroom. In the 1960s, Lillian started enclosing a four-page, black-and-white catalog in orders, eventually expanding these catalogs until they were the major advertising and source of orders. The company now publishes eight full-color catalogs for different product niches, including "Christmas Memories" and "Lillian Vernon's Kitchen."

Today, Lillian Vernon Corp. in New Rochelle, New York, boasts more than 20 million customers worldwide. Some are famous. Singer Frank Sinatra ordered a monogrammed lint remover. Former First Lady Barbara Bush and actor Arnold Schwarzenegger are also customers.

Though Lillian Vernon Corp. is now publicly traded, Lillian remains the chairperson and chief executive officer of her company.

"Generally," she says, "those entrepreneurs who see beyond their creativity and learn how to read the barometers of growing a profitable business have an excellent chance of success."

# 37.

## EVERYTHING COSTS
## MORE THAN YOU THINK

How much money do you think you need to
start your business? Double it.

■ ■ ■

Lawrence Rouse quit his job in Illinois in 1978 and moved to Kansas.
His plan was to run three companies for a client while he built up his own
financial and management consulting firm.

"Timing was bad," Larry says. "The economy went down the tubes,
and my client sold his businesses. I hadn't had enough time to establish my
own practice. I had $1,500 in my pocket. It was ugly."

Larry moved back to Chicago, where he knew relatives would at least
feed him, and started doing subcontracting work for other consultants.
That was the inauspicious beginning of Associated Enterprises, Ltd., now
located in Lakewood, Colorado.

The company took five years longer than Larry anticipated to get roll-
ing because he tried to start on a shoestring budget, with little working
capital to carry him through that unexpected financial loss.

"I wasn't totally stupid, but bad timing caught up with me," Larry says.
"Almost inevitably it takes longer than you think to get established, and just
when you need to make a professional impression, you run out of advertising money, clean suits, and business cards."

As fast as he could, Larry built a cash reserve earmarked for emergen-
cies only. He now keeps at least three months of operating capital in the
bank at all times because he never knows when unexpected expenses will
come up or the economy will go down.

Larry knows his start-up experience isn't unique because half his practice now consists of finding financing for young companies. The other half
is business valuations, expert witness services for legal action, and general
consulting.

"I'm working with a client now that is a successful, $20 million company, and it's strapped for cash," he says. "Every time [company management] opened a subsidiary, it should have set up a reserve fund for unexpected expenses."

Each industry is different, but Larry advises his clients to build up enough money to pay their bills for at least two months. Many of a company's customers don't pay for 30 or 60 days, so even a bustling business has to survive until the cash flows in.

"When I was still in Chicago, a major phone center went out for six months," Larry recalls. "For companies totally dependent on their phone systems, this was terrible. It was three or four months before they got any money back from the phone company. By then, some were out of business.

"You never know what's going to occur."

When the economy booms and Larry's business grows, he starts planning for the next downturn. He stocks up on letterhead stationery and office supplies. He leases rather than buys computers to conserve capital.

Larger companies keep lines of credit. Larry has a $1,000 line, but also maintains several credit card accounts.

"A lot of companies are not prepared," he says. "They wake up one morning, need money, and they've never met their bankers."

Larry tells his clients to force their banks, if necessary, to allow them to meet with bank officers, then send the officers quarterly financial statements.

"So when you need a loan, you don't have to start from scratch," he says. "You have someone who understands your company."

He also tells start-ups to hire financial advisers used to working with small businesses.

"The small-business accountant will do the same work as one used to working with established companies and will call to warn that your quarterly taxes will be due next week or ask why a particular expense was so high last month."

# 38.   NICKEL AND DIME
## TO DEATH

The detail costs of starting a business,
in time and money, will exceed your
expectations and patience.

■ ■ ■

**T**om Pray worked 12 rebellious years for a large engineering and manufacturing conglomerate; but he got frustrated with not being listened to. "That's when I knew I wanted to own a business," he says.

Tom saved the earnings from real estate investments to start a corporation. At the same time he quit his job in 1995 to find a new venture, the bank where his wife worked was sold and her job was eliminated. The Prays then bought Better Home Systems, a Lake Forest, California, company on the decline. The firm installed in-wall stereos, central vacuum cleaners, and other low-voltage systems in luxury houses.

Even though Better Home Systems was an existing business, the Prays had to spend $25,000 in start-up expenses before they earned a dime in revenues. The expenses were crippling in the first two years.

Although the company was located in California, Tom incorporated in Delaware, which cost $1,500. Then California demanded $1,800 for this "foreign corporation," as the state called it, to do business in Southern California. In addition, Tom had to pay several hundred dollars to get his general contractor's license. Then he paid several hundred dollars more for a separate license to install security systems. That second license also required him to pay to be fingerprinted and photographed by a law enforcement agency.

"Every time we turned around, there was another fee to pay or permit to get," Tom says. "I couldn't believe all the details."

California is one of the more burdensome states for start-up businesses. However, most states and communities have fees, licenses, regulations, and restrictions that add to the costs of hanging out a business shingle. Few first-timers anticipate the weight (and *wait*) of this gauntlet.

But that's hardly the end of it, Tom says. The company he bought already had a phone system, a copier, and an adding machine. In addition, he had to buy a personal computer and accounting software. Tom was for-tunate. Many companies require far more equipment.

Tom's does most of his work through new-home builders, many of which require their subcontractors to have their own bonding, liability, and worker's compensation insurance. If his company sells the electrical systems it installs, it must have a resell permit for collecting sales and use tax. If he has employees, Tom needs state and federal tax identification numbers for payroll taxing purposes.

"It's endless," Tom says. "We thought we could start this with $10,000. It cost $25,000 before we made any money."

The Prays put their entire life savings into the business and lived on credit until the revenue started flowing. "That caused cash flow problems because we paid high interest rates on the credit card debt we incurred," Tom says.

Shortly after buying Better Home Systems, the company's lease expired and the Prays had to move. What Tom initially perceived as a problem turned out to be a blessing.

"We discovered that we didn't need nearly the amount of space we had been renting," he says. "When we moved, we were able to work out a shared-space situation with some friends who own a business and needed additional warehouse space.

"The move cut our rent in half and our commute from 45 minutes to 10 minutes," Tom says.

The experience taught Tom that cutting costs can be as much of a money-making opportunity for a company as growing revenues. Fortunately for the Prays, the economy in general and the new-home market in particular were improving as they plunged into business ownership. They finally paid off their personal debts in 1998, but are still paying off the business's previous owner.

"The only way to make it work is to be willing to risk everything," Tom says, "and that includes every dime and minute you've got. Probably more."

# 39. BIRD IN THE HAND

Having contracts in hand before starting
your business gives a tremendous
boost to success.

■ ■ ■

Carl Bailey had owned a variety of small businesses when he noticed that many large companies and organizations were looking for specialty items with strong identification value. He decided, in 1993, that custom-made ties and scarves bearing a group's logo or name were ideal for this purpose.

A product supplier can go broke waiting for retailers to pay for merchandise.

"At first, I had a lot of inventory out on the street," Carl says. "I'd walk into stores, and my ties would still be on the rack. I'd be having a heart attack."

He should have started J.C. Neckwear & Scarves, located in Philadelphia, Pennsylvania, with enough orders in hand for 6 to 12 months' operating capital, Carl theorizes.

"That would have taken unnecessary pressure off, so I could devote time to seeking new contracts and completing current contracts," he says.

Carl explained his lack of a capital cushion to his banker, who was willing to arrange a line of credit, and to his suppliers, who were willing to give him better credit terms and flexibility to bring in some revenue before he had to pay their bills. Carl also changed his focus so that now he deals strictly on custom orders. He doesn't have any up-front inventory manufacturing or storage costs.

"I sell the ties before I make anything," he says.

Too many fledgling entrepreneurs start their ventures before they find out whether anyone wants what they have to sell, says Carl, who does volunteer business counseling with minorities.

"What I tell people to do before they start is test the market," Carl says. "Go to people who will be your customers, and see if they will buy what you have."

The double benefit of up-front orders is receiving start-up operating capital and gaining market research that validates your business concept. Some people will make valuable comments that help you clarify your idea, modify your product or service, or hone your target market.

However, asking would-be customers to pay for product before you have any is tricky. To compensate, you must have a carefully crafted concept and some samples. You also should research the most likely buyers.

Carl learned that private clubs, country clubs, and universities are receptive to his custom ties and want to buy them in quantity. This knowledge is important to his strategy of obtaining sales before manufacturing product. It wouldn't be cost effective to produce a handful of ties.

Carl also discovered markets within markets: not only did the University of Pennsylvania want custom ties, the medical school and business school wanted their own unique designs. And when an exclusive men's club in Washington, D.C., admitted its first women members, representatives from the organization sat down with Carl to design a club scarf to complement the custom ties J.C. Neckwear & Scarves already provided.

"My business is really made by being creative with customers' ideas," Carl says. "At first, I paid someone else to design the ties, but my manufacturer said the best touch was to do it myself. Now I know what to look for in design."

Always looking to expand his knowledge and efficiency, Carl took computer graphics courses to learn how to create his tie and scarf designs using modern technology.

"I'm not that artistic," he says. "I'm proof that anyone can take a business, no matter what it is, and make it a success if they are willing to put in the time."

# 40.

## LIVE WITHIN
## YOUR MEANS

Every start-up business benefits from
following a realistic budget.

■ ■ ■

The recession of the early 1990s gave Maureen Murphy two options: relocate or start her own mail-order catalog consulting firm. Because owning a business had been her dream, Maureen chose the latter, establishing Murphy Marketing in Santa Monica, California, in 1995.

Maureen had an idea how much her revenues would be and what expenses she would incur, but she did not create a realistic business budget at first. That was a costly mistake. Even a home-based consulting practice had greater expenses than Maureen imagined. She had wrongly assumed she would live on less.

"I overspent at the beginning, partly because I didn't realize how fast my start-up capital would be depleted just with basic expenses," she says.

However, Maureen didn't make the additional mistake that so many start-up business owners do: she didn't ignore her financials. She didn't have to ignore them—she didn't believe them.

"For the first year, every time I reviewed my expenses, I would say to myself, 'But this isn't my real budget. I will spend much less once I've gotten this kicked off,'" she says.

Maureen underestimated most expenses, especially taxes. She also aimed too low for her revenue goals. Although this seems to be a happy mistake, unrealistic revenue goals, based on underestimated expenses, can hold a company back.

"There was no reason to set such modest income goals," she says.

Maureen finally put her business spending and income on a simple bookkeeping software program.

"I figured out my actual costs instead of just what I thought [they were]," Maureen says. "I could see that I wasn't being extravagant, and that I wouldn't get by on less money eventually. I had to increase my revenues."

Now she reviews her business cash flow and other financial reports monthly and, for an overview, annually. From past experience, Maureen can forecast future expenses.

"When I really knew how much I needed to earn to survive and to flourish, I took the steps to earn the money," she says. "When I began to target higher financial goals, I started achieving them."

Without an accurate budget, Maureen's initial approach to her business was skewed. She started consulting in all areas of direct mail advertising, because she thought her areas of expertise, mail order and cataloging, were too narrow to sustain her business.

Over time, Maureen has discovered that although her market has fewer catalog firms than companies using direct mail to generate sales leads, the catalogers need her skills more on an on-going basis. These long-term contracts are more lucrative than one-time projects. She also found she could command higher pay in a specialized area than in trying to serve everyone in direct mail.

Maureen, like many consultants, has found that client demands for her knowledge exceed the time she has to give. Therefore, she created a monthly forum through which she coaches professionals in the mail-order industry. Also to maximize the use of her time, Maureen teaches classes and seminars in mail order and cataloging.

"A financial consultant looked at my results and called them wildly successful," she says, "but I think I can still make quite a bit more by getting more on-going projects and [giving more] classes."

# 41. CASH IS KING

A new business must create cash flow
to survive. Even profitable businesses
fail if they run out of money.

■  ■  ■

**W**isconsin is known for cheese and football and ginseng. You don't believe it? Paul Hsu didn't either in 1972. The native of Taiwan's Pescadore Island was well acquainted with the gnarly brown root that the Chinese have used for centuries to cure everything from anemia to insomnia. Then a friend showed Paul an article stating that 90 percent of American ginseng is raised in Marathon County, Wisconsin.

"My mom was ill. Bearing 14 children had taken a lot out of her. So I sent her two pounds of American ginseng," says Paul, who was working as a social worker for the state of Wisconsin at that time. "My father wrote back—they didn't have a phone—six months later and said Mom's health was improved. She slept better, walked better."

That convinced Paul to start Hsu's Ginseng Enterprises, Inc., a part-time ginseng distribution business, and plant his first ginseng crop in 1973.

The good part of ginseng farming is the $45 to $65 a pound Asians will pay for the crop. The bad part is that the farmer must invest as much as $125,000 an acre and wait four years to harvest a crop. And land can be used only once to raise ginseng.

Now *that's* a cash flow headache.

"No cash flow can kill a business," Paul says.

Most fledgling business owners don't realize that even a profitable company can go bankrupt without cash flow. Profit is an accounting principle. You pay your bills and employees with cash, not profit. Furthermore, you must have the cash at the right time. If you must pay workers each week and your bills each month, but your customers don't pay you for 60 or 90 days—or four years, in Paul's case—the business has a cash flow lapse that you must plan for.

Cash forecasting is a record of known expenses in future months. That record helps the new business owner avoid overspending whenever a big check arrives, only to starve a month later when the annual insurance premium is due. Without such planning, the company misses profit opportunities, hurts its credit rating, and eventually goes bankrupt.

To give himself cash flow until his own crops matured, Paul started selling ginseng raised by other farmers.

"I borrowed from my mother-in-law, friends, relatives. Five years later, I was finally able to get a loan," Paul says. "Now I have a line of credit, so I no longer have cash flow problems."

Most Americans buy Chinese ginseng because it's cheaper than the American counterpart. Paul looked toward Hong Kong, Taiwan, Singapore, Malaysia, and China, where Wisconsin ginseng is prized because it's stronger.

"North American ginseng has a light, bitter taste with a touch of sweetness; it has a more herbal flavor," he says. "I believe those differences make North American ginseng a saleable alternative across the Pacific.

"Exporting also helps a domestic company weather periodic economic downturns," Paul says.

Paul's strict control of costs and cash flow helped grow Hsu's Ginseng Enterprises into the United States' largest ginseng exporter, with annual sales of $20 million, almost a third of the total U.S. ginseng exports. The company owns a thousand acres, although it cultivates only 160 acres at a time. Hsu's Ginseng Enterprises has 220 employees in ten offices in five countries.

"Most people don't realize the commitment in time and effort a small business requires," Paul says, "and the stomach for risk."

Thank goodness for the antistress characteristics of ginseng.

# 42. COUNT THE BEANS

### Track your inventory closely. Don't keep anything that's not covering its costs.

■ ■ ■

After owning a liquor store, Larry Thompson decided to try his hand at a more sober business: gourmet coffee. He bought a Coffee Beanery franchise in a Newark, Delaware, regional mall in 1990. With just 764 square feet of space in the store, every inch had to yield maximum profitability.

At first, Larry served brewed drinks and sold packaged coffee and tea, coffee makers, bean grinders, mugs, and other accessories. However, the merchandise mix was wrong, and his inventory costs were too high—52 percent of sales.

Typically, if a business's costs are too high, it either prices its merchandise higher or reduces its profit margin. Larry probably could have gotten away with the first strategy if his were the only gourmet coffee shop in town. But supermarkets, discount stores, convenience markets, even gas stations sell gourmet coffee, Larry points out. He couldn't price himself out of the market.

Some business pioneers have covered mistakes in their cost of goods with higher prices. For example, the first video stores sold blank videotapes for $18. Eventually, however, sharp-penciled competitors entered the market with better cost controls and captured sales with lower prices, driving the high-priced stores out of business.

The other option—lower profit margins—might work for a business with large volume, but a small shop won't produce a living wage if it lowers its profit margin too much. And nobody's in business to do that, at least not for long.

To get a handle on his costs and what merchandise was profitable and what wasn't, Larry set up his cash register to separate all his products into categories: coffee makers, grinders, and drinks served over the counter, which he broke down into subcategories such as café caramels and espresso-based drinks. This practice is common in retailing. Larry learned it from a grocery store where he worked while in college and later used it in his liquor store.

At the end of each month, Larry got a printout that told exactly how much of each category had sold. He discovered that tea accounted for less than 2 percent of his sales. He didn't sell many coffee makers, and after the first months, bean grinder sales dwindled.

Many retailers try to achieve a certain dollar volume in sales per square foot. They reduce or eliminate merchandise that doesn't meet their goals. Based on the Coffee Beanery's inventory tracking, Larry says, "We cut back on the tea we carried. We reduced the number of grinders we carry from three to one, and we don't sell coffee makers at all anymore. That provided more space for packaged gift sets. We sell 50 types of coffee beans."

Beverages are now 60 percent of sales, compared with 40 percent in 1990. Cost of goods dropped from 52 percent to 39 percent. Larry's shop is the number one franchised location among more than 200 for Coffee Beanery.

For a single-location store whose owner works in the business, monthly is probably often enough to evaluate costs and inventory, Larry says.

"I'm here, so I get a feel for costs," he says. "And talk to the customers. They'll tell you what's selling."

However, customer habits can vary widely with location. Other Coffee Beaneries are located in airports, on streets, and in shopping center kiosks that are even smaller than Larry's shop.

"A street-front shop will sell more packaged foods, like sandwiches, than I do and may carry only 12 types of beans," he says.

A business owner also can use sales and inventory information to market the business, Larry says.

"My cash register can tell me how many eight-ounce cups I sell to mall employees. Should I run specials on that? Should I push 12-ounce cups? Should I give mall employees mugs so they'll be traveling ads for my business?

"Having the information is great, but you must evaluate it, too," Larry advises.

# *43.*  PART I:
# KNOW YOUR PRICE

Price your products to make a profit.
It's difficult to raise prices later.

■ ■ ■

Trish Kasey was a human resources manager, but when her daughter was born in 1991, Trish wanted to stay home with her. Inspired by Amy Dacyczyn, publisher of "The Tightwad Gazette" newsletter, Trish decided she could publish a newsletter for moms, whether they worked or stayed at home.

"I had absolutely no idea what to charge for subscriptions," she says. "Instead of researching how much it would cost to produce [my newsletter, I researched] comparable newsletters. They charged $12 to $15 a year, so I figured I should charge $12."

Trish overlooked the fact that those other newsletters were published quarterly, and hers was a monthly.

The first edition of "Mommy Times," published in Trish's Newport Beach, California home, hit the mailboxes in 1992.

Trish had no idea whether she could make any profit at $12 per subscription. And after the publication grew from four pages to ten pages, she couldn't.

She also learned that she couldn't keep subscribers if she raised her prices—not because her newsletter wasn't worth it, but because people had already been persuaded that it was worth $12 a year.

Price is an elusive number, but you should figure it out before you start. Then show a sample of your product to some potential customers and ask whether they would be willing to pay your price. If not, and you can't cut your costs or are unwilling to cut your profits, you shouldn't start the business. It's as simple as that.

Here's a simple formula for calculating your price for a product. Multiply the cost of material and labor times the number of units you want to make each year. Add all other costs. Add your desired profit. Divide the result by the number of units. The answer is the price you must charge.

Those "other costs" can be deal killers. For "Mommy Times," they included printing, postage, advertising, delivery costs, office supplies, and sales and income taxes.

If Trish wanted to research the price for "Mommy Times" before she started publication, based on 1,000 expected subscribers, her calculations would have been as follows: Materials and labor of $2 per newsletter cost $24,000 ($2 times 1,000 subscribers times twelve issues a year). Add indirect costs of $36,000. Add a desired profit of, say, $12,000. The total is $72,000. Divided by 1,000 units, this figure breaks down into an annual subscription of $72.

Trish realized she would go broke if she continued publishing "Mommy Times" the same old way. She had to cut costs. When a friend who had a Web site for his real estate company offered to host a "Mommy Times" site on the Internet free of charge to Trish, she jumped at the opportunity.

The site went up in October 1995 (www.mommytimes.com), and the response was huge. The site includes an e-mail advice and comment section, articles of information, and support for mothers.

"I'm reaching thousands of mothers worldwide instead of hundreds across the United States," she says. "We got this reputation of being only for stay-at-home moms, but we're a support network for working moms, too."

The electronic "Mommy Times" makes money by selling products for moms and babies, a virtual mall set up by an Internet commerce in exchange for a percentage of sales. The Internet store requires no inventory, so it adds no up-front costs or interest and warehouse charges to the business. Trish also sells some banner ads at the site.

The May 1996 "Mommy Times" was the final print edition, and the newsletter is now completely an "e-zine," saving printing, paper, and postage costs.

# 44.
# PART II:
# THE VALUABLE INTANGIBLE

Time is more valuable than money.
Be sure to price your time accordingly.

■ ■ ■

**Q**uick Tax & Accounting Service started in St. Louis, Missouri. because of a family fight. Roy Quick, at the time a corporate accountant, wanted to buy a new Macintosh computer. No way! The kids are entering college, and we need the money, replied his wife, Edith, a junior high school teacher at the time. So Roy started preparing tax returns at night and on weekends to pay for his computer and software.

"The first year [1984], we had one client who was my best friend," Roy says.

However, the business soon grew to the point that Roy could quit his corporate job and join Edith full time. The toughest part, they both agree, has been realizing—and charging for—the full value of their expertise and services.

Undercharging and giving away too much service and advice are among the biggest causes of financial ruin for service businesses.

"You want the business so badly, and then clients try to intimidate you into lowering your price," Roy says.

"But it's a big mistake for services to try to be the cheapest," Edith concurs.

In theory, to calculate its prices, a service provider starts with the annual income it wants to make and adds total costs. It then figures out billable hours each year (generally 20 percent to 50 percent less than the hours actually worked). The company divides income plus costs by billable hours. The result is the hourly rate the service provider must charge.

In practice, that hourly rate may have to be modified by competitive pressures. If you don't want to ask competitors what they charge, ask their clients what they pay. Many trade associations keep track of standard industry pricing.

The Quicks finally set a minimum price on tax returns they prepared. If a client balked, the Quicks referred him to another tax preparer.

Roy and Edith also look at the "hassle factor." Clients who are disorganized, require hours of research to complete their tax work, call dozens of time for free advice, and are unpleasant to work with are a hassle and, therefore, more costly to have as clients than organized and friendly clients.

"You must identify your unprofitable clients promptly and change your billing method," Edith says.

After several years in business, Roy and Edith sat down after tax season and graded their clients—A, B, or C. The A clients are lucrative and pleasant. The C clients are hassles, to be replaced by As, if possible.

Some of the bigger clients are the easier ones to work with, the Quicks agree, because they understand the value of ability, experience, and quality, all service intangibles. These clients don't mind paying $200 for returns that save them $1,000 in taxes and don't trigger IRS audits.

At the other end of the scale are clients like the man who was paying 12 percent interest on his home mortgage. When interest rates plunged and Roy suggested he refinance, the man saved $6,000 in interest over the year. However, the client was angry because the lower interest payment reduced his tax refund by $2,000 the next year.

The Quicks have increased their fees over the years, which has driven away a few of the troublemakers. They also added an up-front deposit that the customer must pay at the first appointment.

"Service businesses sell knowledge," Roy says. "Once you've given that away, you have no leverage [to get paid]."

Besides, Edith adds, "If they won't pay you now, what makes you think they will pay you later?"

The Quicks also started accepting credit cards.

"We were amazed how much we liked the results," Edith says. "We don't get bad checks, and the client can't say, 'Oh, I forgot my checkbook.'"

# 45. THE SEARCH IS ENDLESS

Trying to get a bank loan is one of the hardest
ways to finance a business start-up.

■ ■ ■

After earning a business degree and working two years at a health club, 23-year-old Tim Mansour decided, in 1985, to open his own health and fitness club in his home town of Rome, Georgia. He had limited capital, so Tim approached a local bank for a loan. Then a second. Then a third. In all, more than 50 banks turned down Tim's loan application.

"I was asking for a million dollars, and I didn't have a great business plan," Tim admits. Also, bankers were skeptical because Tim was so young, and no one wanted to finance a health club, where 20 start-ups fail for every one that succeeds.

Often, persistence alone does not bring success in landing the financing a new business owner requires. Even today, banks are not great friends of business start-ups, but in the mid-1980s, most weren't even on speaking terms with small businesses in general. Then, as now, bankers want business borrowers to prove their ability to repay loans. That usually requires a combination of experience, collateral, creditworthiness, profitable financial statements, and positive demographics.

Start-up business owners have a tough time proving the worth of their ideas because they don't have at least three years of financial statements to demonstrate that they have been profitable, growing, and generating enough cash flow to meet monthly loan payments.

Tim's attitude was that no isn't an answer; it's just another obstacle. It is significant that Tim tried to learn from each failure. Every time a banker turned down Tim's loan application, he asked why. Then he improved his presentation for the next banker.

"It's not what you want to tell the bank; it's what the bank wants to hear," Tim says. "Each wanted to know what I was planning to do in the next three to five years. So I added that. Then it wanted to know what I would do if I got into trouble."

Finally, one banker suggested Tim contact the U.S. Small Business Administration (SBA).

Since 1953, the SBA has guaranteed small-business loans made through banks and other commercial lenders. The government takes on some of the perceived additional risk of lending to smaller companies. But the SBA, too, wants evidence that loans will be repaid. In the 1990s, just a fourth of SBA-guaranteed loans nationwide have been made to start-ups.

"I don't think I ever would have gotten a loan without the U.S. Small Business Administration," Tim says.

With the help of a professional loan packager, Tim sharpened his concept so that he wasn't proposing just another gym, but a multipurpose fitness complex with swimming pools, racquetball courts, outdoor sundecks, childcare, weight rooms, cardiovascular machines, aerobic studios, lockers, steamroom, sauna, and whirlpool. Tim would own the building. The business would compete on service and facilities, not on price.

One of the smartest things Tim did while searching for a bank loan was to research his industry and the entire Southeast. A hometown friend suggested he try Gwinnett County, an Atlanta suburb, which was one of the fastest growing areas of the United States during the 1980s.

Research, a good business plan, and persistence finally paid off. Tim got an SBA loan to open the first Fitness International with three employees in Snellville, Georgia, in 1986. It was a 25,000-square-foot freestanding facility that grossed $650,000 in its first year.

That club and a second one Tim opened in 1988 enabled him to pay off his SBA loan in five years. He took out another SBA loan for his third center in 1991 and built a fourth in 1994. The last three centers are almost double the original's size.

The company now has 200 employees and grosses $4 million a year. After building another five to eight Fitness Internationals in the Atlanta area, Tim plans to take the concept national. However, he expects to finance future expansions through private partnerships with wealthy investors.

"Having an excellent track record with the original health complex made funding the additional three complexes not as difficult," Tim says. "But it's still tough, even with 12 years of successful experience."

# 46. EQUITY, NOT DEBT

Debt financing can stifle growth for a start-up
firm because repayment of debt is a
considerable drain on earnings.

■ ■ ■

After 25 years' experience in financial institutions, Frank Shemanski gave up his senior executive position to launch Southwest Financial Services, Inc., in Brea, California. The company leases merchant credit card equipment and processes credit card purchases. It charges a 1 percent to 2 percent fee for each transaction in which a client accepts a credit card for payment.

Frank knew the industry and the job before he started his company. He had worked for banks of all sizes and created a financial services division for one employer, not unlike starting a company. However, when he began Southwest Financial in 1988, he didn't have the deep pockets of a major corporation, so Frank borrowed $20,000 from family, friends, and long-time business associates. Like many entrepreneurs, he didn't want to give up any ownership or control.

But debt financing was a big mistake that drained limited resources, Frank says. For example, he was paying 8 percent to 15 percent interest on the loans.

"Using debt instead of equity resulted in paying interest on money that we had not yet put to work generating income, thus creating an expense that affected profits and diluted net worth of the company," Frank says.

In addition, the initial capital gave an illusion of wealth that the start-up company did not yet have. Southwest Financial paid salaries equivalent to corporate jobs and bought business equipment and furnishings that did not generate income.

"We quickly recognized that we were expending capital at a faster pace than the revenues were being generated, so we immediately tightened our financial belts, obtained additional funding to replace the excesses, and monitored our results on a daily basis," Frank says.

He went to his initial debt holders and asked them to convert their loans to equity in the company. All agreed because Frank could demonstrate that for a little more risk, they would likely get higher returns on investment as the company continued to grow.

The change boosted Southwest Financial in two ways: The company no longer had to use income to pay interest and principal, and the extra equity improved the company's net worth on its financial statements.

"Tight management, effective planning, and a lot of long hours and hard work got us over the hump," Frank says.

Frank now advocates running a company with the help of both a business plan and a budget based on the amount of investment capital available. These documents help the owner resist the temptation to spend money on products and activities that do not contribute to making money. New business owners, especially those who have been used to the perks of high executive positions, are tempted to lease fancy offices, equip them with lavish furniture, and pay themselves high salaries. A budget helps an owner differentiate between what the company must have to survive and the luxuries that will have to wait.

After righting the ship, Southwest Financial has enjoyed double-digit growth each year, processing more than $100 million in purchases a month. The company has been profitable for ten straight years. While retailers have been the backbone of the $500 billion credit card industry, the company benefits from large numbers of manufacturers, distributors, and even government agencies that now accept credit card payments. Secured purchases on the Internet are another growth segment. Also, Frank contemplates taking Southwest Financial public, which would provide liquidity to his initial investors and a source of new money for the company.

# 47. INVESTIGATE BEFORE YOU BORROW

Allow plenty of time to research all the
options for equipment financing.

■  ■  ■

**A**fter a decade of publishing specialty magazines, Jane Weyhrauch sold her company with the idea of staying home.

"It drove me crazy; I got pneumonia three times," she says. "I have to work."

Rather than return to publishing, Jane thought that the printing end of the industry would be simpler. In 1992, she founded Deluxe Color Printers, in Newport Beach, California, a short-run and medium-run, four-color digital printing operation.

Before she could begin operations, Jane found good used equipment at a great price in another state. She made a $40,000 down payment to the seller, believing that she could then use the equipment as collateral for a bank loan. Jane was wrong. Most bankers don't understand the printing industry, she says, so they don't want to make large equipment loans at all. They were unswayed by Jane's ten years of previous business ownership experience.

Jane finally found a mortgage lender that would make a $190,000 loan at 12 percent interest. However, after the seller packed the equipment on a truck headed for Deluxe Color Printers' plant, Jane's lender suddenly went out of business. She had three days to find alternative financing.

"I was groveling. I had to find the money, or I'd be out of business before I started," she says.

Jane wound up paying almost 20 percent interest on the loan she found, which cost her $50,000 in interest over five years.

"I should have spent more time researching options for an equipment loan," she says. "I should have investigated the lender more carefully, but it had been in business a long time and had a good reputation."

Part of Jane's problem was timing. Many lenders failed in the early 1990s. However, she says if she had looked harder, she could have found other lenders familiar with the printing industry.

The importance of finding a lender that specializes in your industry can't be overstated. Lenders, as well as investors of all types, are more flexible and patient in industries they understand.

Jane says she would have started by contacting trade associations, which often know from their members the names of qualified lenders with industry knowledge and experience.

"Then I would have started making calls to everyone I knew in the industry and asking questions," she says.

The press turned out to be a good investment, Jane says. It was still worth more than half its selling price and in good condition after Jane paid it off. However, she is more careful about her purchases of high-tech film-developing equipment and a second, larger printing press. Deluxe Color Printers must keep up with the newest technology to survive in a fiercely competitive market and industry, Jane says.

One-fourth of the printers in the area when Deluxe Color Printers started are now out of business, Jane says. Deluxe, on the other hand, has grown 20 percent in each of the past two years and now has 18 employees. One key to Deluxe's survival while others have failed is Jane's close scrutiny of equipment financing. Jane won't even take out a loan to buy certain equipment, such as computers. And she won't lease them for more than three years.

"They're obsolete as soon as you get them," she says. "Figure that you have to make money on them immediately because they won't be worth anything at the end of the lease.

"A lot of people want to spread their payments over many years, but they're kidding themselves," Jane says. "They are not saving money."

# 48. A PIECE OF THE ACTION

Even if you're willing to give up part of your
venture to gain working capital, you may not
find any takers. Figure out an alternative.

■ ■ ■

Jim Dartez was an engineer by training and a medical instrumentation salesperson by experience when a large conglomerate approached him about saving one of its divisions that made water quality monitors. What he found was a money-losing manufacturer with stagnant growth and disgruntled employees. The entire industry suffered from unreliable technology for monitoring the quality of water that waste treatment plants and water companies didn't trust.

Jim proposed a three-year turnaround plan that involved moving the division to New Orleans, Louisiana, and starting from scratch with new employees and new technology. Just as he started implementing the plan, another company began buying up the conglomerate's stock. So, in 1987, Jim and his wife put every dime they had into buying the division to create Royce Instrument Corp.

"I should have given up some of the company to have cash to work with," Jim says. "We would have grown faster, though it might not have been better. Outside investors tend to micromanage. They don't know what you're doing, but they do know their money is at risk."

Keeping such investors informed and happy takes management resources, Jim says. Entrepreneurs must weigh the financial largess against this time commitment. On the other hand, a company gets a tremendous lift if the owner can attract the right investor with expertise in finance, marketing, or the venture's needed technology. Many private investors, who made their fortunes building companies before cashing out, look for companies that need their knowledge as well as their money.

But even with diligent searching and good professional relationships, most entrepreneurs can't find this type of investor.

"I was so ignorant about finance, I probably would have danced to any drum around. But no one was beating the drum. No one had confidence in what I was doing. It's good that I didn't run into someone from the Mafia at the time," he jokes.

Instead, Jim and his wife risked everything. When Royce Instrument ran into financial trouble because it did a poor job collecting receivables, Jim's wife stepped in to correct the problem. However, Royce Instrument's basic problem ran even deeper than unpaid receivables. In the mid-1980s, water quality monitoring instruments were so poorly designed that customers hated them. Therefore, Jim hired aerospace and telecommunications engineers who knew nothing about water and everything about developing monitoring instruments. They applied techniques from other industries to create new water analyzers.

Their work would take two years, however, and in the meantime, Royce Instrument had to survive on its revenues because Jim didn't have any cash reserve.

"We were selling ratty old stuff that wasn't very great—although it was as good as anything else on the market—but we really supported our customers and replaced things that didn't work," Jim says. "When our new instruments came out, our customers were willing to try them because we had done a good job for these people."

By 1991, Royce Instrument's portable analytical instruments became the U.S. benchmark for reliability and accuracy in water quality monitoring.

Even before that time, however, Jim was aware that global markets, in addition to U.S. markets, would be important stabilizers for his company in the 1990s and beyond.

"When you have an economic lapse in one part of the world, other areas are strong or in flux," he says.

Now more than half the company's instrument sales take place in 50 foreign countries. Jim's goal is for international sales to account for 60 percent of Royce Instrument's business.

# 49. DON'T GIVE AWAY YOUR BABY

### Venture capitalists will take a large chunk of ownership for relatively little investment.

■ ■ ■

**G**ia McNutt didn't want to own a business; she just wanted to serve her customers. She worked for an equipment reseller that supplied Hewlett-Packard. When that reseller went out of business, Gia took her customer base, including Hewlett-Packard, to another reseller that wasn't used to giving the lavish customer service that she had been trained to deliver.

"My customers kept telling me they really wanted my service, but I never would have started my own company without my husband," Gia says. Lawrence McNutt, who had owned other small companies, was the entrepreneurial one, she explains.

The McNutts had no money to start Special Order Systems, a computer reseller in Rocklin, California, that would have to pay for goods sometimes 30 or 60 days before their customers paid the McNutts. So when a venture capitalist offered Gia $150,000 for 20 percent ownership, she was ready to bite.

"We were desperate. It was the money we needed," Gia says, "but my husband said, 'No way!' Now I thank my lucky stars we didn't take the deal."

Actually, Gia and Lawrence got a better offer than most start-up entrepreneurs who seek venture capital. This money source isn't even available for the vast majority of business start-ups. Venture capitalists look for fast-growth companies in industries with which the investors have had a lot of experience. Fast growth to a venture capitalist means 40 percent a year or more. They also want companies from which they can pull out their profits—typically by going public—within five to seven years.

Many venture capitalists demand a much greater percentage of ownership than the McNutts encountered. Typically, venture capitalists value a company's worth more conservatively than the entrepreneur does. They then base their percentage of ownership on that capitalization. Special Order Systems' investor valued the company at $750,000. The McNutts thought it would ultimately be worth many times that amount.

Venture capitalists generally figure that two of every ten investments they fund will be strikeouts, two will be home runs, and six will be base hits.

Gia launched Special Order Systems in 1992 with ten credit cards, which paid her bills until customers paid her. She had to monitor this juggling act carefully to avoid paying high interest payments on unpaid credit card balances. After several months, suppliers were willing to extend trade credit to Special Order Systems.

"We did exactly what we promised we'd do, so they became more comfortable working with us," Gia says. "Even today, we get more trade credit than our balance sheets warrant because we are such good customers."

In addition, at Gia's request, one large company agreed to speed up its payments to Special Order Systems, which greatly eased cash flow.

"It really wants to see small companies succeed. I can't say enough about its support," Gia says.

From the beginning, Gia realized that computer products were becoming more standard, regardless of manufacturer, and their sales were increasingly competitive. That combination would shrink the profit Special Order Systems could make from product sales alone.

"Therefore, we built into our business plan [our goal to] become a value-added service company," she says.

Now Special Order Systems strives to be a one-stop supplier of everything from systems design to hardware to software to training. Services do not require the up-front investment in inventory that products do, so the strain on the company's limited capital is less.

"This is a more profitable future for our company as computer software and hardware become commodities," Gia says.

The formula seems to be working. Special Order Systems has doubled in size every year and grossed $8.3 million in 1997.

# 50. WHAT'S WRONG WITH A MILLION-DOLLAR CONTRACT?

Companies that are developing new
technology should bring in outside investors
early in the start-up process.

■ ■ ■

**A** long-term goal of starting their own company sent Joyce and David Freiwald on a long-term mission to develop the needed management skills. Their research told them that lasers would be one of the fast-growth segments of technology, so Joyce took a job in business development for a research and development company in the oil industry. David ran a laser division for a large defense contractor. When that company decided to bail out of the laser project, the Freiwalds decided it was time to start their own company in 1992. F2 Associates uses lasers to remove coatings, such as paint or glue, from large surfaces. The process is environmentally safe.

"We sold our house in San Diego, California, moved to New Mexico, and used our severance pay to start this company," says Joyce, who became president of the new venture. David became vice president in charge of technology development.

F2 Associates quickly earned multi-million-dollar contracts from the Department of Energy and the Air Force. The agencies wanted a demonstration of the effectiveness of the company's technology. Those contracts would appear to launch the new company toward certain success. Instead, they propelled F2 Associates into the awkward adolescent stage. In building their management and technology experience, Joyce says, they overlooked the need to understand how the financial game is played.

"I wish that I had known earlier about the process, problems, and players in raising capital," Joyce says. "I could have avoided a lot of expensive mistakes."

The usual bank loans were not appropriate for high-tech firms like F2, she says. The amount of money the company needed to commercialize its technology was too large to raise from friends, family, and individual investors. Economic development programs in small states like New Mexico were inadequate for the technology firm's needs. And venture capital groups worked in narrow niches, so finding the right fit was time consuming and difficult.

"Some investor groups want to be in before the technology is developed. We developed the technology before trying to get outside investors," Joyce says. "At that point they want to see commercial sales before they invest.

"One investor group would say, 'You're too mature for us.' And another would say, 'You're not mature enough.' And investors have niches within technology. They want biotech or software; we're neither."

Venture capitalists, many of whom manage funds for individuals, pension funds, and insurance companies, look for industries in which they are experienced and knowledgeable. Not all specialize in high-tech sectors; some like retailing or consumer products. Regardless of the industry, these professional investors look for high growth, typically 30 percent to 50 percent a year, in companies from which they can pull out their money by selling stock to the public within five to seven years.

The typical venture capitalist reads a hundred business plans for each one he invests in. Venture capitalists and wealthy private investors rarely put their money in companies that don't come highly recommended by experts they trust, like attorneys and accountants. Many of these experts make lucrative livings by playing matchmakers for cash-hungry young companies.

"You have to kiss a lot of frogs," Joyce says. "I have learned to avoid the middlemen who want to be paid up front or to be paid a monthly fee in return for their help in seeking capital. I will work only with those who are willing to work on a contingency basis."

In 1998, the Freiwalds gave up majority ownership of F2 Associates to an investment group, which used a shell corporation to take the company public. That status gives investors a market in which to sell their shares if they want out and gives the company greater credibility with financial managers. The financing also helped the company pursue strategic relationships with major companies that have the markets established for the laser cleaning process. The Freiwalds remained to run the company.

"It wasn't my first choice," Joyce says, "but we needed to do something to raise the millions of dollars needed to commercialize the technology."

# 51.

## DIGGING OUT OF EARLY HOLES

An undercapitalized start-up has to beg and
borrow to keep the company afloat.

■ ■ ■

In the mid-1980s, Gail Johnson was a college nursing instructor yearn-
ing to do something more meaningful with her life. Then Gail met a couple
who had built their lives around their new baby daughter. When the infant
was diagnosed with a susceptibility for sudden infant death syndrome, they
could not find childcare willing to take responsibility for the little girl.

"The mom was so upset, and I thought there was no reason to feel this
kind of pain," Gail says.

She decided to combine her nursing skills and love of children to establish a childcare program that would serve children both with and without
special health needs. Gail's attitude was positive: Her father had owned a
fuel oil company when Gail was a teenager. Her husband owned an engineering firm. If she wanted to start her own business, well, of course she could.

Gail's husband did the design work for her new venture, and his company absorbed many of the prestart-up costs Gail otherwise would have had
to pay. One of his business associates, a real estate developer, agreed to
finance construction of the building, which Gail would repay through rent.

Rainbow Station opened in Richmond, Virginia in 1989 with 18 children. It needed 95 to break even. Then the economy took a nosedive.

"My husband could no longer afford to absorb my costs," Gail says. "I
remember thinking, 'Oh, my gosh! What have I done?'"

Gail used her two MasterCards and some savings bonds to try to save
the company. As each new child enrolled, the money went to pay the bills.
But after six months, Rainbow Station was broke.

Gail tried to renegotiate her lease, pointing out that her rent was far
more than the market rate. The landlord said that was the price she had to
pay for his up-front financing.

"Finally, he said he'd evict me, and I said, 'Do what you have to, but I
can't pay,'" Gail says. "I knew he couldn't use the building for anything
else because it had been built to our specifications."

In the end, they worked out a deal to add the unpaid rent to the end of Gail's lease term.

In addition, Rainbow Station had to pay exorbitant liability insurance rates because of the special nature of the clientele. The first-year premium was as much as the company would later pay for three childcare centers, once it had established a safe track record.

Rainbow Station survived financial starvation "only by the grace of God and a never-say-die attitude," Gail says. Fortunately, the childcare provider met a huge need in the Richmond area, and Gail had done a good job marketing its services to working parents. By the end of the first year, the center had 117 students, enough to pay the bills.

Demand was strong for Rainbow Station's blend of accredited early childhood education and registered nursing staff. At the grand opening for the first center, the owner of an office park offered to give Gail land for a dollar if she would build a second center in the park. Gail went to the phone book and started calling banks. When she got to the "Ns," a young loan officer at NationsBank agreed to visit Rainbow Station.

"She became our advocate and, I found out later, the sole reason I got the loan," Gail says.

The second Rainbow Station was 90 percent filled within nine months. The third and fourth were in the black immediately.

"None of this has been easy," Gail says. "You have to be willing to move forward in spite of obstacles.

"Never give up."

# 52. SPEED KILLS

A company that grows faster than expected
can have as many money woes as
an undercapitalized firm.

■ ■ ■

**M**ichael Downes learned a great deal about making printed circuit boards and contract assembly while working as an executive of a large international computer manufacturer. But that company was on a starvation diet, selling off most of its facilities and slashing staff by 90 percent.

In 1992, when Mike had the opportunity to buy one of the company's factories in Methuen, Massachusetts, at a fire sale price, he jumped at the offer. The plant designed and made printed circuit boards for its corporate owner, grossing about $2 million a year. Mike figured he could do better by offering to make printed circuit boards for many electronic manufacturers.

Mike's pro forma financial work showed that his new company, which he named Tri-Star Technologies Co., would gross $9 million in its first 12 months. However, his certified public accounting group balked. Tri-Star couldn't do better than $7 million, the number crunchers insisted.

Tri-Star sales were $11.5 million the first year, growing to $18.7 million in three years.

The uninitiated would think that's great. It's not, Mike says.

"When a company has exponential sales growth, the incoming cash flow is less than that required for the next month's expenses, even when you are profitable," he says. "Although profitable during the first three years, Tri-Star was 95 percent financed by debt, and because of the time involved to bring on new financing, money was always available two to three months after it was really necessary."

Mike recommends that the entrepreneur preparing to launch a new venture develop financial projections based on a normal, expected growth rate, a worst-case scenario, and a better-than-your-wildest-dreams result. Then go out and find financing for the middle point.

"This will limit your trips to the financial well," he says, and if performance exceeds normal expectations, "you have time to line up additional financing."

Ironically, dwindling competition among independent circuit board manufacturers boosted Tri-Star business even more. The number of U.S. shops declined from 2,000 to fewer than 700.

At first, Tri-Star only fabricated the boards. Quickly, it evolved into designing, assembling, and testing circuit boards made to the specifications of many electronics companies. These customers then asked Tri-Star to do contract assembly work.

The new contract assembly services stretched Tri-Star's bank account more than Mike expected. Plus, pricing was inaccurate, making some assembly projects unprofitable.

"Contract assembly is an unbelievable cash drain," Mike says.

Growth that is too rapid strains more than a company's finances. Expansion taxes the company's human talent, often demanding of them skills and decision making for which they are unprepared. It also puts pressure on equipment, internal processes, and customer relationships.

To resolve Tri-Star's difficulties with rapid growth, Mike went on the hunt for an equity investor. He studied Tri-Star's pricing models either to make each activity profitable or to get rid of it. And, finally, he beefed up his management team.

"One person cannot do it all," Mike says. "If you consistently assess your talents against your future needs, you can avoid placing subordinates in positions that place them over their heads, the proverbial Peter Principle."

**36.** The numbers really do matter in running and growing your business. Take a class, read a book, and make your accountant explain your company's financial statements.

**37.** Create a contingency fund before you start a business. Replenish it as you go.

**38.** Add to your financing projections the taxes, licensing fees, and myriad other expenses your new venture will face.

**39.** Approach your most likely customers before you start your company, and ask for contracts. This will give you an extra financial push in the beginning.

**40.** List all the expenses of starting your business. Modify your list, based on experience—weekly at first, then monthly.

**41.** Don't commit to huge expenses that will drain precious cash until reliable income exceeds company needs for operations and growth.

**42.** Break out the costs and sales of each product or service. Don't forget to include a share of overhead. Dump the money-losers before they drag your company down.

**43.** Know your real costs of doing business. If you must run in the red to beat your competition, you'll never survive.

**44.** Value your time as your most precious asset. You can always make more money, but you can't make more time.

**45.** Create your company with the management experience, collateral, and profit potential that bankers demand, or find another source of financing.

**46.** Include interest costs of debt financing in your business planning so they don't cripple company growth.

**47.** Equipment at a bargain price is just half the equation. Search for or negotiate lease terms your company can live with.

**48.** A piece of something is better than 100 percent of nothing. Share your venture with understanding investors.

**49.** Don't be so desperate for capital that you give away too much ownership and control to investors who don't share your vision.

**50.** The real trick is not just finding capital, but getting it from the right sources in the right sequence. Before accepting investments or contracts, consider their impact on other money sources.

**51.** If your start-up is undercapitalized, be prepared to beg and bargain. It's not the easiest way to run a company.

**52.** Figure out your wildest dreams for your company; then develop a plan to cope with them.

# PART 4

# MANAGEMENT ISSUES

■ ■ ■

You really know that you're a business owner when you make management decisions without looking around for someone else to tell you what to do. It's harder for some to make these decisions than others.

Your business will become the accumulation of management decisions you make. The suppliers will be the ones you find. The distributors will be the ones you woo. The business will accomplish its work under the guidelines you set up.

When you make your management decisions, adopt the as-if principle. If you act as if you are the owner of the most polished, professional, significant company in your industry, it will tend to be the truth. If you act as if nobody would buy from you—the person who flunked third grade math and never so much as served as hall monitor—that will tend to be the truth, too.

However, the fact you must never forget is that just because you're the owner doesn't mean you should be the sole decision maker. Your customers are the ultimate judges of your management decisions. So base your decisions on how you want your customers to see your products and services. Your decisions should always strive to satisfy and serve the customers.

# 53. COUNT THE HOT DOGS

Institute inventory control
measures from the start.

■ ■ ■

If you look at CKE, Inc., today, with its more than 4,000 Carl's Jr., Hardee's, Taco Bueno, Rally's, JB's and Galaxy restaurants, it's hard to imagine the whole conglomerate started with a hot dog cart.

Carl Karcher had an eighth-grade education, a steady job as a bread truck driver, and burning ambition. On July 17, 1941, he borrowed $311 on his Plymouth and added $15 from his wife's household budget to buy a hot dog cart in Los Angeles, California, across the street from a Goodyear tire factory. Carl sold hot dogs, chili dogs, and tamales stored in an ice chest and heated on a steam table. His first-day sales totaled $14.75. A muffin tin served as the cash register.

Carl kept his bread delivery job, and even though his wife, Margaret, often worked the cart with their first baby asleep in the Plymouth parked next to the cart, they had two employees run the stand. Each man worked alone for an eight-hour shift, earning $12 a week. Carl arrived at 2:00 am each night to collect the day's receipts and close up by stacking sheets of plywood around the cart.

Soon Carl noticed that the night shift consistently made about 25 percent less than the $12 to $15 that he expected. When he stopped by the cart unexpectedly one evening to study the problem, he discovered the employee was using hot dog buns that Carl hadn't bought.

The employee, who confessed his scam, knew that Carl tracked inventory by counting the buns, which Carl purchased by the dozen, instead of the hot dogs, which he bought by the pound. The employee bought his own buns and used Carl's wieners and condiments to sell three dozen hot dogs "off the books" each shift, pocketing $3.60 per day.

"I learned fast about food costs and inventory controls after that," Carl says. "To this day, I place integrity high among the traits of a good employee."

Nowadays, employee theft is an even bigger problem for American businesses than it was in the pre–World War II economy. Accurate recordkeeping and inventory control are important tools for curbing employee theft; however, today's small-business owner must do more.

Begin by comparing every check returned with the business bank statement to the general ledger. Examine the amount of each check, the signature on the check, and the endorser on the back. Unless you do all the record-keeping, bill paying, and product ordering yourself, assign these duties to different people. And because many thefts and embezzlements are uncovered when the culprits aren't around to keep the scheme going, require employees to take regular vacations.

Inventory management serves an important purpose beyond keeping employees honest, however. Good inventory control helps an owner avoid overbuying while keeping the best-selling merchandise in stock, and it eliminates slow-moving products.

Obviously, much more is at stake today with CKE's inventory. Carl switched from hot dogs to hamburgers and other food just a few years after starting the company. The business has grown by opening its own restaurants and by franchising. In 1997, CKE added Hardee's fast-food chain to its stable.

Today, CKE has 40,000 employees and $1.2 billion in sales, making it the fourth largest hamburger fast-food company in America. Although Carl is now chairman emeritus, he still rises at 5:00 AM and goes to the office every day.

# 54. IT'S A BUSINESS; ACT LIKE IT

Hide your self-doubts; your business will
become the professional image you project.

■ ■ ■

**B**arbara Ward gave up her career as a daily newspaper reporter when her daughter was born in 1975. She contemplated how to make some extra cash at home, but home-based businesses weren't yet trendy. Even big offices didn't have voice mail, personal computers, or fax machines.

"I wasn't looking for a big success, only extra income while I stayed home with my infant daughter," Barbara says. "I knew nothing and just plunged ahead."

That was the foundation for Ward Public Relations in Upland, California. Her first client was a local business association that hired Barbara to produce a newsletter.

"I went home and told my husband, 'I just got my first client. Now all I have to do is figure out how to do a newsletter.' I had no idea," she says.

Attitude is a big part of success. The world takes business owners as seriously as they take themselves. Even in pursuit of her first clients, Barbara adopted a can-do, professional attitude.

"I was shaking, but I didn't let them know that," she says, and soon other corporate, government, and school clients followed.

One day, the top executive of one of Barbara's clients called to complain that he had trouble reaching her by phone. Phone answering machines weren't sold in every drug store and shopping mall back then, so Barbara bought one through a specialty supplier for $275 to answer the telephone when she wasn't able to.

"I realized this really could be a business, so I'd better start treating it like one," she says. "I got a separate business phone line, which no one had back then. I paid big bucks for professional-looking stationery and got business cards. I put my daughter in nursery school three mornings a week so I could make business calls without a baby crying in the background."

And she never, *ever* told people that Ward Public Relations was headquartered on a card table in her kitchen.

Barbara became involved in a professional public relations organization, which taught her a great deal about her industry. Originally, she accepted any job for which people would pay her. She designed shopping bags for a jewelry store and penned a gem-of-the-month blurb. She wrote radio commercials and press releases. Gradually, she realized she liked best her public relations work with public agencies and focused on signing those clients.

Part of acting like and becoming a truly professional business owner is having the confidence to turn away unsuitable or undesirable projects and clients.

"Stay true to yourself and your own beliefs," she advises. "Don't get sucked into somebody else's ideas of how to do business."

Barbara's turning point in this regard came in the mid-1970s when she had one client she hated working for.

"We really needed the money, but I finally decided that when my contract was up, I wouldn't renew it," Barbara says. "This was so great. Never again was I going to do something just for the money.

"That's when I started getting more challenging projects and bigger clients."

When her husband, Mike, retired from the *Los Angeles Times,* he joined the business full time, too. Barbara no longer hides the fact that they own a home-based business. No one is shocked; some are envious.

As the office world has changed, Ward Public Relations has had to change, too.

"I was talking with the attorney for one of my clients in 1989," Barbara remembers. "She said, 'Fax that document to me.' And I said, 'I can't.' She said, 'Barbara, how do you expect to be a serious business person if you don't even have a fax machine?'"

Barbara immediately ran out and bought one.

# 55. BREAK THROUGH BARRIERS

The marketplace isn't eager to let
new businesses into the game.
Expect to fight for your foothold.

■ ■ ■

As a receptionist in the governor's office on the island of Guam, P. June Terlaje watched many Japanese couples come to the U.S. territory to get married. Companies that arranged these trips were owned by Japanese men who seemed oblivious to the brides' need for help with their gowns, hair, and makeup, June says.

A former hairdresser, June dreamed of opening a total salon where brides could be pampered and prepared for their weddings from head to foot; however, Oriental tradition dictated that brides leave for the ceremonies from their homes. So, instead, June opened Island Wedding Service in Tumon, Guam, in 1983 to coordinate weddings and receptions.

June wanted to tap the lucrative Japanese wedding market, where well-established travel companies served as booking agents for these large celebrations.

"I had a very difficult time getting any bookings because I was a woman, non-Japanese, and a new business," she says. "I was green, and I had no references."

Adding to her woes, June spent most of the $80,000 she had to start her business even before she opened the doors, leaving nothing for marketing.

New business owners often encounter roadblocks erected by established competitors. Initial planning ought to identify these challenges, as well as potential ways over, around, or through the barriers. Occasionally, an entrenched competitor succeeds in building impenetrable roadblocks to competitive entry, usually by obtaining patents, locking up suppliers, or signing exclusive contracts with buyers. But that's rare. In most industries, a newcomer can find some niche toehold to get a start and then build on.

In the beginning, Island Wedding Service worked with local brides to survive. However, June kept marketing to the Japanese travel services.

"I needed a male front," she says. "My husband, Henry, would have to take leave from his job with the Guam police department to go to these meetings with me."

June pursued the Japanese market for two years before she got a break.

"I had a very professional brochure made, and I went to Japan to try to get in to see some of these travel companies without an appointment," June says.

At one company, she had laid her brochure on the receptionist's counter when the company president walked in. He looked at the brochure, then went to his office without saying a word.

"He didn't even talk to me, but he saw how professional that brochure was, so he told his office manager to give me several bookings to see how I did with them," June says.

That first contact led to bookings with numerous Japanese wedding travel companies. Island Wedding Service handles as many as 200 weddings a month, earning the nickname "the drive-through wedding company."

Over the years, June continually added services, such as providing flowers, photography, and tuxedo rentals. Now Island Wedding Service handles every detail of the wedding event to avoid giving any bit of the business away to competitors.

The industry is so competitive, June says, that Island Wedding Service must keep an eye out for competitors' spies who pose as friends of her clients just to collect information on how she runs the business.

Island Wedding Service added a general sales office in Japan in 1998 to attract even more Japanese weddings. June's daughter joined that office after earning a college degree in management, and June's two sons work in the Guam headquarters.

To expand, the company sought more weddings with Guam brides, who were its original market, and worked to apply its event-planning experience to large parties other than weddings.

"These are ways to add stability and strength to our company," June says.

The services also help stymie any new competitors that might get their own toeholds in hopes of eventually dominating the Guam entertainment planning market.

# 56.

## MAKE YOUR YARDSTICK

Set goals so you can measure the company's
progress and health at critical early stages.

■  ■  ■

Kenneth Jacobs was content to be an employee of a large security company until the owner prepared to sell it.

"I saw the handwriting on the wall, that the company would go through major changes," Ken says. "I was 37, and I thought if I ever wanted to try something on my own, this was the time."

In 1987, Ken started JMG Security Systems in Fountain Valley, California, to install burglar alarms and other security devices. Within two months, he had an ulcer.

"I was so used to a healthy paycheck, and here I was with zero income and worrying about money and paying bills," Ken says. "Rather than worry day in and day out, I decided to set some performance goals for the next six months, then reassess where I was at that point."

The only significance of six months, he says, was that he had enough money to live on for that length of time.

"I didn't know if six months was long enough, but it gave me enough time to get my name out there and attract some clients," Ken says. "It was a mental game, but it totally relaxed me and freed me up to do my best work."

Some entrepreneurs fret about what goals to set. To start, they might use industry standards. Some trade groups keep track of performance averages. Dun & Bradstreet Corp. annually publishes *Industry Norms and Key Business Ratios,* which gives typical financial statements and key ratios, such as current assets divided by liabilities or annual net sales divided by inventory, for major Standard Industrial Classification (SIC) codes. This book is available in many public libraries.

To Ken, however, the goal itself wasn't as important as the act of setting it. The important step was to have a benchmark against which to measure performance.

"How do you know how you're doing if you don't have anything to measure your performance by?" he asks.

Ken determined he wanted 10 percent of the security alarm business in his area within five years.

"I had no idea what that meant," he says. "Now I know that 2 percent is a huge number. I can tell you I'm a significant player in the field."

Initially, Ken wanted to make sure JMG Security Systems was increasing its revenues and adding accounts—the right kind of accounts. By his standard, this meant larger commercial clients that don't shop based only on the lowest price and that pay their bills on time.

"I couldn't do that at first, but I wanted to make sure I was moving in that direction," Ken says.

At the end of six months, Ken sat down with his wife to decide whether JMG Security Systems was reaching its goals.

"If yes, we would go forward; if no, then we wouldn't sink more money into it. We'd be smart enough to look for something else," Ken says.

The Jacobses gave their venture the go-ahead, but Ken acknowledges now that if the company hadn't been moving in the right direction, closing it would have been a tough decision.

After the first year, Ken never questioned JMG Security Systems' viability. He deliberately pursued and won well-known accounts, such as Nordstrom department stores; Edison International Field, the baseball stadium of the Anaheim Angels; Knott's Berry Farm; and Home Depot stores throughout Southern California.

"Once you have one of these plums, no one questions your credibility," Ken says. "I have outlasted all my major national competitors."

# 57. FORMAL INSTRUCTION

Classes, seminars, and tapes on business
management are invaluable aids in
launching a business.

■ ■ ■

**R**on Schmitz grew up on a farm, but he was a born carpenter. The first purchase he ever made, at the age of 16, was a table saw.

Ron decided college would bore him; however, he did attend two years of trade school in carpentry before he got the opportunity to buy a run-down cabinet shop in Sauk Rapids, Minnesota, in January 1975. He was 23 years old. Shortly after he took over, he had to fire the man who was to show him how to run the business.

That initial year, Ron's Cabinets, Inc., had revenues of $80,000 and two employees. Ron took care of the customers, while his wife, Dianne, handled the finances.

Although Ron knew the technical side of cabinet making, he knew little about business. He didn't have experience with taxes, personnel, business management, or marketing.

"I should have gotten some formal education in business before buying [the company]," Ron says.

In fact, his lack of business knowledge almost lost him the business.

"In the first two years, it wasn't a question about profitability," Ron says. "I would do anything just to break even so we didn't lose the place."

The turning point was an advertisement that came in the mail for a series of seminars on business management. Ron and Dianne went to the introduction to get a free dinner. They couldn't take the time and money away from the business to attend such a long, expensive course, but Ron bought the audiotapes, which covered much of the same information.

"That turned me around; I learned so much," he says. "I would listen to tapes on the road to jobs. I listened to them 10, 20 times."

After that, Ron signed up for every short course and seminar he could find on business topics. He figures he has attended thousands of them over the years. Because he couldn't take a semester off from running the business, Ron concentrated on one-hour, three-hour, and one-day workshops. Also, he sought out successful businesspeople and asked endless questions.

"They usually are willing to share information," Ron says.

Ron recommends tapes by Brian Tracy and Zig Ziglar and seminars in insurance, personnel issues, taxes, marketing, and basic how-tos in running a business.

Ron's informal yet unrelenting education paid off. By 1979, Ron's Cabinets had grown so much, it moved into a larger building. Ron invested in new technology, such as computer-aided design and engineering. He developed a highly integrated production and management team. The company won awards for its quality.

Finally, in 1997, when Ron's Cabinet's sales topped $7 million, Ron sold the company. His brother's death from a heart attack at age 47 a short time earlier had been a wake-up call for Ron. He had many other endeavors he wanted to pursue; none of them was in business. In addition, the timing was right, Ron says. Interest rates were low, potential buyers were plentiful, and businesses sell best when they're doing well.

"Besides, the business was growing, but I didn't want to take it to the next level," Ron says.

He did, however, continue to attend seminars and listen to business tapes until the day he sold the company.

"Over the years, I found that people who don't need the information that much are always [at the seminars], and those who need it most aren't," Ron says. "Always continue your education as long as you want to succeed in business."

# 58. THROUGH OTHERS' EYES

Always look at your company through a
new customer's eyes to identify areas
that need improvement.

■ ■ ■

**W**hen Robin Dickinson stepped in to run Construction Notebook News in 1995, the family business was on the ropes. Her father-in-law and the company's owner, Robert Dickinson, had died in 1993. His widow, Sheila, was trying to keep alive the trade newspaper and construction plan clearinghouse for Las Vegas, Nevada.

Robin didn't know publishing or construction, but she did know how to run a business and read a balance sheet. Years of helping her father operate a casino and a mortgage company had given her the experience she needed.

Suddenly, however, Robin was the 37-year-old boss of employees in their 50s who didn't want to listen to a newcomer. She heard a lot of "we've always done it this way," and Construction Notebook News was slowly dying on that status quo path.

Publishing, construction, and Las Vegas were all changing. Construction Notebook News had to be reborn, too. Experts told Robin the paper version would soon be obsolete. Others told her that traditional plan rooms, where contractors went to view blueprints before bidding on jobs, would be obsolete, too.

Whether starting new or starting over, "Look at the complete company as a new customer does," Robin says. "It forces you to see glaring mistakes and keeps you focused on a direction of positive change."

The reason for taking a new customer's view is that existing customers are almost like friends. They know more about your company and products or services than is apparent on the surface. They're more forgiving because you've done a good job for them, maybe even carried them through tough times. They're so familiar with you that they hardly notice if your company is getting old and tired. New customers presume that what they see is what you are.

Although being the new kid on the block made her management of employees tough, it gave Robin a fresh perspective on the company. She was closer to the mindset of that proverbial new customer. And what that new customer would see at Construction Notebook News was a company without management for two years. The customer would see a dated-looking publication with pricing too low for sustained profitability. The customer would see time wasters and money wasters.

"I brought in an aggressive, hands-on accountant who would tell me what to look for on the financial side of the company," Robin says. "Then I worked at every job in the company for three to six months so I knew first-hand how to do that work." At any point, she can step in and do a job, keeping the operations flowing smoothly.

"I talked with every department head and said, 'Now you're accountable.'"

Robin knew customers wanted a better-looking publication, so she changed the layout and typeface of the *Construction Notebook News,* which runs 150 pages a week. She also updated the computer software, making production easier and faster.

Robin believed the newspaper's 1,500 subscribers would be willing to pay more for the publication's useful information, legal ads, and job postings, so, in increments, she increased the subscription rate from $295 a year to $445. Circulation remained steady.

Robin also knew that a growing number of contractors, engineers, and builders had access to the Internet, so she put the entire publication and blueprints for job bidding on a Web site.

"In five years, we might be able to do away with most of the paper, but maybe not; people still like to carry it with them," Robin says.

Robin made each change logically and slowly, she adds. "I explained to the affected employees what the change was, why it was necessary, and how it changed their job. Then I'd ask, 'Will you try it?' They did."

# 59.    ASK, DON'T THINK

A successful business must focus on
what clients want rather than on what
the owner thinks they should have.

■ ■ ■

After three decades working in various businesses, Jim Collison became the founding executive director of a statewide employers' group in Iowa in the 1970s. In 1981, he acquired the organization by assuming its $30,000 in debts. Jim then changed it to a for-profit business and renamed it Independent Small Business Employers of America, Inc. (ISBE).

Organizations, whether nonprofit or for-profit, don't fall into debt by accident.

"It took me years to overcome my compulsion to sell what I knew with certainty that bosses needed and concentrate on what they wanted," Jim says. "The worst reason to invest time, money, and energy into a business is because *you* are in love with the concept or the product or the activity. Unless enough potential customers or clients like what you offer well enough to pay for it, your business is doomed."

The association started as a lobbyist for employer issues, working on political issues with lawmakers.

"Frankly, that's not what most employers, managers, and supervisors today care about," Jim says. "Besides, the National Federation of Independent Business and U.S. Chamber of Commerce dominate the political arena like Wal-Mart dominates retailing."

ISBE members consistently called Jim in his Mason City, Iowa, office for advice and guidance on employee-related problems. Finally, the light dawned, and Jim dropped the lobbying.

"We put our energy into helping bosses deal with what they want most: to avoid headaches and to achieve more when dealing with employees."

Business associations have many opportunities to sell products and services on behalf of other companies. In fact, these groups must have such sales because they can't live on members' dues alone. Jim receives several offers a month for a 1 percent to 10 percent royalty or fee if he will promote to ISBE members such items as insurance, credit cards, long-distance telephone service, computer software, overnight shipping services, bill-collection services, and equipment leases.

However, Jim will not accept any of these items unless his members strongly indicate they want it through surveys in the group's monthly newsletter, *Smart Workplace Practices*. He also asks visitors to ISBE's Web site for comments, experiences, and ideas. Because of members' interest, ISBE does offer group health insurance, but few other products and services.

"Recently, a consultant was trying to interest me in doing a story in the newsletter about why employers need to offer their employees the new benefit he is marketing. I told him, 'I agree that employers and their employees need what you have, but I have strong doubts that they want it.'"

Jim has used members' comments to guide many of his business decisions.

"For years, we offered members an employee handbook writing service," Jim says. "But custom-written employee handbooks are expensive, and few employers want to pay the kind of fee that's needed for a well-written handbook."

When Jim would give a $2,000 or $3,000 quote for a handbook, many employers would gasp and say something like, "I was thinking more like $200." So, finally, he put together *The Complete Employee Handbook Made Easy,* with 300 pages of 101 policy topics, including 240 sample policies. The $239 price is more popular with members.

Through continual tweaking, Jim has built ISBE to more than a thousand members in 40 states. In addition to the handbook and monthly newsletter, Jim and his staff of 12 provide telephone and fax-back advice and coaching on employment-related issues.

"I recommend you do some kind of market survey before you plunge headlong into your business with all your money or the money of friends and relatives," Jim says. "And continue to survey your market as long as you're in business."

# *60.* NO INSTANT SUCCESSES

Many business owners work years without
taking money out of their businesses.

■  ■  ■

**R**owena Fullinwider loved to make almond pound cakes, jams, and
jellies for holiday gifts for friends or to raise money for local charities.
Soon her foods were so popular that people encouraged her to start her own
business.

"I had no financial background, no marketing or sales experience, limited finances, and no business credit," Rowena says. "In addition, I had no
manufacturing or equipment experience, and the only customers were
church bazaars, charities, and a few store owners who loved the product."

Nevertheless, Rowena did extensive planning, renovated an old warehouse for a gourmet manufacturing plant, and opened Rowena's, Inc., in
Norfolk, Virginia, in 1983. She had one full-time employee and a lot of
nerve.

"God was my copilot," she says. "I decided at the beginning that I did
not have the knowledge to go it alone. Therefore, after analyzing problems,
I frequently gave them up to Him."

To survive during the start-up period, Rowena worked an evening job
as chemist at a local hospital for more than six years while getting the company on its feet. She did not draw any salary from Rowena's, Inc., for four
years so she could make sure her employees were paid.

"I was determined to survive," she says. "I had this thing going, and I
couldn't just walk away.

"I worked all the time," Rowena says. "I gave up community work. I
stopped sewing. I stopped cooking. I had to let many things slide."

Because she was working two jobs, Rowena depended on her employees to share her business vision and help grow the company. She made sure
the employees understood company costs and the need for efficiency.

"We instituted time, motion process, and raw material studies of all products to find [their] true cost," she says. "We then set in place cost reduction

procedures, in some cases dropping the product if it could not be produced and delivered to the customer profitably."

However, Rowena wouldn't delegate certain management jobs. Although she hired a plant manager with an MBA in finance, she actively participated in all financial decisions. Also, she took a college accounting class so she could understand her financial statements. When her manager left after two years, she was able to run the company on her own.

"I grew this business without debt," she says. "I expanded my line of credit each year to cover growth, but I paid it off early each year, which pleased my banker.

"I undertook an aggressive reading program, scanning the literature for applicability to my business and sharing valuable information with the appropriate team members," Rowena says.

She networked continuously in the community and her industry to gain more knowledge. She helped found the Food and Libation Association of Virginia to provide food manufacturers like Rowena with networking, information, and shared advertising opportunities.

Gradually, over the years, Rowena was able to cut back her hours at the hospital until she finally quit. Rowena's, Inc., eventually moved into an 8,000-square-foot warehouse with a factory and small retail store. Sixteen full-time and 45 seasonal employees fill orders within 48 hours. The products are sold mostly through 3,000 gourmet stores and gift shops and to gift basket manufacturers.

Although people thinking about going into business shouldn't underestimate the amount of work and sacrifice ahead, that shouldn't stop them, Rowena says.

"When you want to go into business, you have a choice: gather all your information and go forward or do nothing," she says. "My advice is just move forward."

# *61.* BIG GAME HUNTING

Start-up companies often work with less than
ideal customers before winning large accounts.

■ ■ ■

After graduating from high school, Dan Zettler worked for a machine shop, where he invested hundreds of hours of his own time to master computer-operated machines that could create tiny parts for watches and other products. That preparation paid off. When Dan was just 22 years old, one of the machine shop's customers asked him to create a prototype for an electronic component. In 1988 Dan left the shop to start Zet-Tek to manufacture electronic contacts and medical components in Anaheim, California.

"At first, we dealt with little companies because that was our only choice," Dan says. "We wanted big companies, but their buyers didn't want to take the risk to hire us."

Unfortunately, some of these small firms were cash poor. They paid their bills 90 days or 120 days past due. A couple of them went bankrupt, owing Zet-Tek money.

"We lost $1,500 or so, which was a lot in those days," Dan says. "That might be our profit for the month. I couldn't take a paycheck when that happened."

Dan remembers trying to get a contract with an international office equipment manufacturer. "I would have done anything to get in the door at that company," he says. But the buyer told him that the company was reducing its vendor list in his category from 22 companies to 5.

A few entrepreneurs start with one or more large corporate contracts, but most, like Dan, scramble to attract larger, more financially stable accounts. It can take years of persistence in contacting corporate buyers and hard work at building the kind of reputation a big company wants in its suppliers. It helps if the start-up has a unique product or service that the large corporation cannot or does not want to provide for itself. It also helps if the entrepreneur researches extensively the corporation he's targeting in order to contact the right people, understand the company's procedures, and ferret out the company's specific needs.

From the beginning, Zet-Tek was known for quality and precision; however, the recession of the early 1990s made it difficult for Dan to attract the bigger accounts he wanted in order to grow Zet-Tek. He had to build his track record through smaller contracts first.

Fortunately for Dan, purchasing managers frequently move from job to job in his industry. Buyers for existing Zet-Tek clients continually moved to similar jobs at other companies in the area. When they did, they usually gave Dan contracts with the new companies because of the quality work he did for them previously.

Zet-Tek's quality workmanship, relationship building, persistence, and staying power through tough economic times slowly paid off. Many of Zet-Tek's competitors went out of business or were sold during this period.

"It took six years to prove ourselves this way," Dan says.

Dan also has found that it doesn't pay to pursue an endless stream of new corporate accounts at the expense of his existing customers. As Zet-Tek has grown to ship $500,000 in finished parts each month, Dan has been careful to service established customers' needs first.

"We have told some people that we're not accepting new customers because we're maxed out at this factory," Dan says.

However, he is also able to cut off business relationships with those late-paying customers who hurt Zet-Tek's finances. This way, he says, his customer base becomes more lucrative over time.

This growth strategy recently brought Dan the ultimate compliment: The international manufacturer whose business he would have died to acquire in 1988 invited him to become one of its vendors.

# 62. CUSTOMER NIGHTMARES

### Your troubles won't be over when
### you get your first customers.

■ ■ ■

Ted Hunter's family had worked in construction for three generations, but 1989 seemed like a good time for Ted to switch from building real estate to building computers. Ted launched Downtime, Inc., in Brunswick, Maine, to specialize in developing and servicing computer networks for companies of all sizes. While real estate and computers seem very different, "the basic principles apply to all businesses," Ted says.

The late 1980s and early 1990s weren't good times for start-ups in many industries. The economy dragged, and business capital was scarce. Few companies were building, but neither were they buying computer networks.

"My first three clients were absolute disasters," Ted says.

One was a consignment store that closed suddenly. The owner skipped town without paying Ted. The second was an accountant who paid his bill slowly over several years. The third was a comic book store that went bankrupt. Ted was never paid for this job either.

"And this was after doing all the research and figuring how to pay the bills," Ted says.

Such stories aren't unusual. Even with the best-laid plans and market research, new businesses have a tough time attracting their first customers or clients. Most accept less than ideal assignments to start. Some don't adequately check the creditworthiness of these first accounts, but even if they do, things can go wrong.

Ted did not allow his initial clients to ruin his business or his attitude. He had enough resources to carry him three years, if necessary, without drawing a paycheck. He learned the necessity of controlling costs from his grandfather, who kept the cost estimate for every construction job he ever bid.

Ted broadened Downtime's base to several industries and types of customers. Construction was an important source of clients initially; today, it is less than 8 percent of his business. Ted has more shipping and transportation clients.

Downtime builds computer networks and sells components to end users. For example, the firm networked the computers of ten Wal-Mart stores. But end users are no longer Downtime's only market. The company also is a subcontractor for assembly houses that have contracts with major manufacturers to assemble and install networks.

"We put together the computer system and the software and make the customized software work," Ted says.

Although more than a third of computer systems sold today are customized, few are bought directly from the manufacturer because they go through these value-added intermediaries, Ted says.

Customers always come and go—sometimes without paying—no matter how old or sophisticated a company is. For example, Downtime had a contract with one of the largest computer manufacturers to service computers under warranty. That manufacturer then signed a nationwide repair deal with a large consumer electronic retail chain.

Such fickleness is why small companies need a mix of customers, products, and services.

It is also important to keep in close contact with clients, Ted says. Downtime has 16 employees, yet Ted himself continually visits customers to stay in touch with their needs. Occasionally, he works at one of their sites, perhaps manning the customer service phone line for a day.

"I don't buy a thousand computers from them, so I'm not at the top of their minds; I have to stay in their faces," he explains. "I give them a day of my time free, and it puts me in touch with the field."

This kind of handholding is a lot of work, but it probably ensures that Ted isn't surprised by the client who skips town or goes bankrupt before Ted suspects anything is wrong.

# 63.    WHO'S NEXT?

Succession planning is essential to save
your company if a key executive dies
suddenly or suffers debilitating injury.

■ ■ ■

Connie Kostrzewa was a preschool teacher in 1982 when her father, Val Kostrzewa, told her that he planned to buy a bankrupt Saginaw, Michigan, machinery company with eight employees. Connie grew up in manufacturing—her dad and grandfather started a company in their garage when she was a child—but she had gone into teaching to assert her independence. Connie was interested in the new venture, however. She sat in on planning meetings and started taking college business classes.

Val bought Miles Machinery with his two brothers and renamed it K-Miles Co. Val was the only one actively involved in running the company when he died 11 months later.

The company was to go through some wrenching problems because of the sudden loss of leadership. The company faced continued financial insecurity and economic volatility because it hadn't planned for such a possibility. Also, it lacked key-man life insurance, which is designed to help companies pay inheritance taxes and other costs when an integral employee dies.

"There was a desperate need for someone to step in and run the company because of all the bank loans taken out to buy the company," Connie says. She already was working at the company during summer break. Following her father's death, she took a leave of absence from teaching and finally made her commitment to the company permanent.

Shortly before Val's death, Dale Wright, a long-time business associate, merged his engineering firm with K-Miles to create Wright-K Technology. Dale helped the new special-order machinery manufacturer grow to 37 employees.

Then, nine months after Val's death, Dale died.

This time, Wright-K had key-man life insurance; however, the company lacked a succession plan and had to totally reorganize its internal operations and corporate goals.

The family persuaded another long-time Kostrzewa business associate, Dick DeYoung, to come out of retirement to become president. They asked Robert Floeter, who has been a salesperson for Val for 31 years, to become sales manager.

Eleven months later, Dick became seriously ill and had to resign. Again, the company—already losing money—had to reorganize.

Any one of these losses could have sunk Wright-K. Inheritance taxes alone put many companies out of business when an owner dies. However, a succession plan is more than just replacing the owner. Its goal is to strengthen the company to meet its needs three to five years down the line. The plan helps a company grow, protects it from loss of key employees, and prepares for the inevitable change that follows such loss.

Ideally, a business owner thinks about passing on the business when she starts the company. Begin *your* planning by developing clear goals and objectives for yourself and your company. Predict potential changes in your industry and individual business; then identify the skills and organizational structure your company will need to meet those changes. Start relinquishing duties to others by training existing employees to fill future needs or by hiring people who can fill these needs. Never assume your children have the talents or interest to take over the business.

In the 1985 reorganization, Robert Floeter became chief executive officer, and John Sivey, who had just merged his manufacturing firm into Wright-K, became vice president. Connie became secretary/treasurer. This time, the company funded key-man insurance policies and set up stock buy-sell agreements.

Today, Wright-K designs, builds, and rebuilds machinery by special order. However, employees never stop training and upgrading their skills. They just never know when they might be called on to assume some leadership role.

# 64.

## THE VIRTUAL CORPORATION

The start-up business can avoid large
overhead costs and remain flexible by using
technology and independent contractors.

■ ■ ■

**R**obert Chesney was sales and marketing director for a Midwest real estate company where one of the firm's part-time salespeople was hugely successful because he used home movies as marketing tools.

"I realized the value of visual aids in selling, and they didn't have to be of great quality," Bob says. "Then a builder asked if I could make one of these videos for him. That lit my fire."

Bob started Chesney Communications in Irvine, California, in 1978 to make marketing and educational videos for companies and entrepreneurs.

"At that time, I had two choices: pay through the nose to rent time at a television station to make these videos or create my own studio," Bob says. He chose the latter.

The firm grew quickly: 25 employees, a large production studio, and all the overhead that went with them.

"If I knew then what I know now, I would have thought virtual," Bob says. "Fixed overhead and large monthly lease payments are like an albatross around an entrepreneur's neck.

"By being flexible and a smart shopper of services and vendors, I can profit from every project by bidding parts of the job out."

Obviously, Bob couldn't buy all the technology in 1978 that makes virtual corporations and home-based businesses possible today, but he didn't have to build as big an operation as he did, either.

"It was chaos personified," Bob recalls. "Every time we turned around, something was broken."

Employee issues also were difficult and time consuming.

"I called a client who was in robotics and asked if he could make robots to operate video cameras," Bob says. "He said, 'Piece of cake.' So, 15 years ago, we switched."

During an economic downturn, Bob cut his overhead even more, taking over many of the production tasks himself by using computers and other software, whose prices dropped almost daily.

Recalling his real estate days, Bob modeled his business after building contractors who bid out every facet of a project to subcontractors. If a subcontractor does a poor job, it loses its contract and doesn't get contracts in the future. These independent relationships, however, must be handled carefully and professionally to avoid Internal Revenue Service scrutiny for treating employees as independents just to avoid taxes and benefits. Even written agreements aren't sufficient to avoid this problem.

Virtual companies like Chesney Communications must issue 1099 forms to independent contractors paid more than $600 in a year and must report the payments to the IRS. They must focus on the specific work to be done, taking care not to tell subcontractors how, when, or where to do the work. Virtual companies should not provide training or equipment to independent contractors. They should pay by the job, not by the hour. And they cannot insist that a subcontractor work exclusively for them.

Within these boundaries, Bob can turn to other specialists, such as graphic designers, scriptwriters, or mailing houses, only when he needs their services. This allows Chesney Communications to employ only three outsiders plus family members.

Now Bob can do much of his production work with a digital video camera, a laptop computer, and a cellular phone. In addition to creating sales videos, CDs, and Web site video clips for others, Chesney Communications has its own library of sales, motivational, business, and computer videos for sale.

"The company has changed only in its utilization of technology," Bob says. "Initially, we had to explain to people what VCRs were. We embrace innovation because it enables us to think small and grow big."

# 65. SCARCITY OF SUPPLIES

If you think money is hard to find for a
start-up business, try finding suppliers.

■ ■ ■

**M**ary Maxwell always had artistic flair. She learned to embroider and
sew as a child; she learned to dance and taught ballet as a teenager. Mary
was 24 years old when she first saw a Victorian lampshade and just had to
make one of these old-fashioned fabric and beaded items herself. Immediately, people wanted to buy one of Mary's creations, so, in 1974, she started
Heart Enterprises in Roseville, California, as an evening business to sup-
plement her day job as receptionist for an aerospace company. When her
son was born in 1985, Mary decided to try to make her custom Victorian
lamp designs a full-time company.

In the beginning, Mary's biggest problem was finding sources of supplies and instruction on how to manufacture the lampshades in quantity.
She discovered the rule of "if it were easy, everyone would be doing it."
Industries with plenty of information and suppliers are highly competitive
and often dominated by large, well-financed corporations. Would-be entrepreneurs are urged to move into uncharted territory. The price for being a
pioneer is time, effort, and persistence in finding the necessary resources.

"I did find a couple of women making Victorian shades for restaurants,
but they wouldn't share any information," Mary recalls.

Mary taught herself to make the shades through trial and error by studying old photographs. She asked thousands of questions at companies even
remotely related to the manufacturing or artistic techniques she was trying
to develop. And when she couldn't find any patterns, Mary designed her
own. She haunted fabric stores looking for just the right silks, velvets, and
other fine fabrics.

Mary couldn't find the lamp frames she needed, so she asked a welder
friend to make some. As business grew and she needed a steady supply of
these custom frames, she got a wire rack manufacturer to produce them. At
first, the company made the frames in off-hours, but the work has grown
into a full production line.

When Mary couldn't find the beads she wanted for the lampshade
fringe, she designed her own and sent pictures to manufacturers asking

whether they could make the beads. Sometimes it took a year to find a supplier. She had to send them overseas to be strung.

Initially, Mary charged just $35 for one of her creations, but as her reputation and work quality grew, her prices increased to $350 and up. Still she had more orders than she could fill. Heart Enterprises does no mass production; each lampshade is one of a kind.

Instead of adapting the secretive tactics of other Victorian lampshade makers, Mary decided to turn her craft's lack of suppliers to her advantage. She made her research and experience profit centers.

"I got over my fear that if I shared, I would lose business," she says.

Mary created three videos on how to make Victorian lampshades and developed a catalog of more than 300 items used to make the creations, from beads to lamp poles. This portion of her business now accounts for 60 percent of Heart Enterprises' revenues, which have increased six-fold in recent years.

As Mary shared her knowledge and sources of supply, an incredible thing happened. Her customers returned the favor.

"People, over the years, have shared their ideas, designs, and techniques," Mary says. "Some customers will call me and give me names of manufacturers they have found.

"If people buy my videos and like making the lampshades so much they want to go into business for themselves, I coach them for free," Mary says. "And I still have as much custom work as I ever did."

# 66. GET THE GOODS ON THE SHELVES

A young company should focus on
gaining full distribution for its products.

■ ■ ■

After graduating from college, Toxey Haas accepted a job as production manager for a food company. However, a steady, corporate career wasn't Toxey's long-term plan. A hunter since childhood in Mississippi, he wanted to develop a better camouflage pattern for hunters' clothing.

In 1986, 26-year-old Toxey created Haas Outdoors, Inc., in West Point, Mississippi, copyrighted his camouflage patterns, and trademarked the name Mossy Oak. Haas Outdoors contracted with a clothing manufacturer to make high-quality hunting apparel, using Toxey's designs.

Toxey's original strategy was to be the Ralph Lauren of hunting clothes, so he carefully limited distribution of his products, which included gloves, pants, jackets, caps and boots. He also limited the retailers that could stock Mossy Oak, allowing them to carry the clothing exclusively in their geographic areas.

"We were so selective with where Mossy Oak was sold that we hurt ourselves," Toxey says. "We built tremendous consumer demand, but people complained that they couldn't find our products."

One reason companies limit distribution is to ensure quality. But Haas Outdoors could produce larger quantities without compromising quality, so the exclusive strategy unnecessarily limited company growth.

"The bottom line for the retailer is that it doesn't need an exclusive territory if we can maintain consumer demand coming into the store," Toxey says.

Haas Outdoors changed its strategy to make Mossy Oak more like Nike, available wherever sporting goods are sold.

"Once your brand is national in scope, quality is not an issue if you have a truly unique product," Toxey says.

A manufacturer must accept its role in attracting sales when distributors and retailers stock its products. Making a quality product is key, but not the only responsibility. The manufacturer must create demand through advertising and provide marketing materials such as brochures the distributor can show its retail clients, as well as in-store displays the retailer can use. The manufacturer also must value the products at a price consumers will pay, which requires calculation of markups for distributors and retailers. The manufacturer may need to include incentives for the distributors' sales forces. After the products get into the stores, it is the manufacturer's responsibility to fill all orders quickly and provide good customer service or, for some products, technical support.

Haas Outdoors' shift toward wider distribution brought its own challenges. For example, hunting is extremely popular in West Virginia, but Mossy Oak sales were low in that state. Therefore, Haas Outdoors opened a factory store in West Virginia that charged regular retail prices, but stocked everything in the Mossy Oak line.

"We did 20 times more business through that one store than we previously sold through wholesale in the entire state," Toxey says. "In addition, the store created great exposure for us. That's a big tourist area, so people bought our clothing, then went home and asked their local sporting goods stores for more Mossy Oak products."

The exposure also brought greater sales for other retailers that stocked the Mossy Oak line.

Now Haas Outdoors' strategy has broadened even more for greater distribution. The company has created a retailing division to develop specialty shopping malls for all types of outdoor sporting products. Another division has created a line of casual nonhunting sportswear called Mossy Oak Companions. A third division produces the company's own television commercials and advertising.

"Everything we do fits in with outdoor sports," Toxey says.

Haas Outdoors is no longer the simple camouflage clothier Toxey envisioned right out of college.

"This rapid horizontal integration has brought back-to-back years of 50 percent-plus growth," he says.

# 67. COPE WITH GROWTH

Fast growth can strain your
company's management abilities.

■ ■ ■

**M**ary Usry was a schoolteacher trained to write grant proposals to bring outside money into her school district. However, when she didn't receive the promised pay for her grant work, Mary took a leave of absence to find out whether she liked being her own boss and could make a living writing grants for nonprofit groups. The answer was yes on both counts, so she quit her teaching job in 1997 to establish Rose Wing Consulting and Grant Writing in Sierra Vista, Arizona.

With the help of the local Small Business Development Center, Mary wrote a business plan. However, it failed to anticipate one thing: the power of word-of-mouth advertising to catapult growth beyond her management capabilities.

"Every time I got a project funded, the phone rang off the hook," Mary says. "I was putting in 20-hour days. There wasn't enough of me to go around, and I missed some key deadlines with my clients."

Mary just hadn't prepared for Rose Wing Consulting to succeed as well and as fast as it did, and she lacked an effective plan for managing the growth internally. It's a common phenomenon among first-time entrepreneurs. You hope and expect that your dream will succeed, but when it does, "it's like juggling eight balls and six of them are on the floor," Mary says. "It's a deadly mistake."

Entrepreneurs who cannot adjust eventually go out of business.

Mary hired two full-time employees, one to manage finances and research and the other to oversee technology and secretarial duties. Both also worked directly with clients, which bolstered Rose Wing Consulting's project coordination. Mary also hired part-timers with expertise in technical writing, information management, and, of all things, calligraphy.

"We put our grant proposals on parchment paper with hand-addressed envelopes," Mary says. "They look different, attractive, and it puts us at the top of the pile" of applications that grant-approving committees receive.

Most significant, Mary assigns each project to a different manager, who establishes a time schedule for all necessary tasks and shepherds the project to completion. When Mary was solely responsible for this oversight, she didn't miss any final deadlines, but did miss a few interim dates that didn't allow the client enough time for revisions.

"We're a team," Mary explains. "I don't put myself in the role of being the boss, except on Monday mornings," when the entire staff meets to update each project and plan the week.

"Everyone needs the scapegoat of a boss," Mary says. "Ultimately, someone needs to step up and take responsibility, and that's what I do. I tell my employees, 'If someone needs to shoulder responsibility, I have broad shoulders.'"

This approach has enabled Rose Wing Consulting to take on more projects without losing control of any of them and reserves ultimate supervision for Mary. She has time to plan the company vision and decide overall management issues, including types of projects to accept and pricing.

Rose Wing Consulting has been able to accept projects coast to coast, from rural health care to urban education. The company keeps costs reasonable for its regular grant-writing work and maintains two pro bono projects at all times.

"I had studied other fund-writing businesses and what caused them to fail," Mary says. "Their up-front fees were structured to include their anticipated total profit. I set [Rose Wing Consulting] up to charge up-front just the cost of doing the project. If [my client] receives a grant, I get 5 percent. If [my client] doesn't get a dime, I break even."

# 68. THE DOWNSIDE OF FRANCHISING

Franchising is not a guaranteed
route to business success.

■ ■ ■

**T**eresa Alexis was working for a nonprofit food bank when a friend told her that a franchise was available for a well-known women's clothing chain. What a great way to go into business, Teresa thought. She didn't have to be a retailing expert or have management and financial experience. The franchiser provided a proven system of doing business, training, established accounts with suppliers, marketing for the chain, and an established reputation.

Teresa researched the company, which had been in business for decades, received a copy of the franchise disclosure document, and had an attorney review the franchise agreement. She opened her shop in Brighton, Colorado, in 1988.

Shortly after Teresa signed her contract, the franchiser was sold to an investment group with little retail background. The franchising company eventually wound up in bankruptcy court, and Teresa's business declined $70,000 in one year. Quitting was not an option because the franchisees couldn't close their stores without the bankruptcy court's permission.

When franchisees signed up, they had to post security deposits with the franchiser in case they went bankrupt. They couldn't get that money back when the circumstance was reversed, Teresa says.

Instead of paying franchise royalties, the stores had taken company merchandise on consignment and paid 10 percent of sales to the franchiser. After the bankruptcy filing, the stores couldn't get merchandise through the company, but if they bought goods elsewhere, they still had to pay the franchiser 10 percent of sales, Teresa says. And the franchising company threatened to sue Teresa for contract interference if she talked with other franchisees.

The franchising company eventually was liquidated, with franchisees getting no money back. Teresa says she lost $60,000. In 1994, Teresa became an independent retailer, renaming her shop Alexis Fashions.

"Most vendors were very good in helping former franchisees establish buying credit with these companies, knowing that the store owners had not defaulted on the debt," Teresa says. Those vendors helped her business survive the transition to independence.

Franchises often are praised for lower failure rates than independents; however, the statistics can be deceptive. If an individual store owner goes bankrupt, but the franchiser manages to resell the franchise and location, it's not counted as a failure.

Teresa says her franchise relationship helped her learn about retailing and buying. It enabled her to build up a clientele that gave her independent store a running head start. However, if you consider buying a franchise, investigate carefully. You and your attorney should begin by reading an up-to-date franchise disclosure document and the franchise agreement. Don't just take the word of a franchise salesperson. In addition, the disclosure document must list lawsuits. Talk to the attorneys for the other parties. The franchiser also must give you names of franchisees. Talk with them, and scout other franchisees. Look in bankruptcy records for names of former franchisees, and take your queries to them. Finally, ask pointed questions about pending changes in the franchising company, including its ownership.

Even with the best franchiser, you have to ask yourself whether you are suited for the franchisee way of life. Do you have an interest and aptitude for the type of business you're buying? Do you enjoy following someone else's set way of doing things? Do you have enough money? Do you realize *franchise* is not synonymous with *easy money?*

Before you've signed your contract, contact other franchisees. Many franchises involve their franchisees in operating committees. Also talk to independent groups include the American Franchisee Association in

Chicago, Illinois, and the American Association of Franchisees and Dealers in San Diego, California.

"I wish we franchisees had been more united and aware of what was going on," Teresa says. "I think a lot of people go into business wide-eyed and innocent and expect people will be honorable. It doesn't always work that way."

# 69. WHO IS BEST?

The key to success isn't necessarily what
you do best, but understanding
what your customers need.

■ ■ ■

**W**hen Carol Lloyd and Thomas Butterworth started Austin Food Tech, Inc., in Anaheim, California, in 1988, Carol was typical of so many first-time business owners: strong on technology, short on management experience. And having worked at Hunt Wesson Foods, even her technology was too specialized.

"I knew everything about ice cream toppings and cone toppings," she says. "Hunt Wesson had 60 percent of the topping market at that time."

Austin Food Tech is a food product development lab that contracts with food manufacturers, bakeries, and even entrepreneurs who think they can make Grandma's spaghetti sauce into the next Ragu. Not many companies needed help developing a new ice cream topping. In fact, in ten years in business, Carol has had only two contracts related to her old niche expertise. That's because she learned to listen for potential clients' problems instead of pitching her knowledge.

"If I had depended on what I knew best, I'd be nowhere," Carol admits.

But Carol's knowledge of chemistry and ingredient interactions had useful applications that food companies needed. For example, in the late 1980s, no-oil salad dressings and similar products were just hitting the supermarket shelves, and they were spoiling too quickly.

"These manufacturers were desperate for a solution to their spoilage problem, so it was a foot in the door for me," Carol says. "Fear sells."

"Cooks may know taste blends, but many don't understand the chemistry going on in food preparation. They didn't realize that when they replaced oil with water in their salad dressing formulas, they needed to add acid to the mix. They checked the pH balance for acidity, but that wasn't enough. That piece of knowledge got me in the door with a lot of companies."

Carol came up with a special low-price program enabling contract food packers to run tests on their formulas to make sure they won't have a problem with spoilage. She developed another program for food entrepreneurs to turn their old family recipes into formulas with ingredients stated by weight which are required for commercial food preparation. Neither is a big money maker, but they do give Austin Food Tech entry into potential long-term relationships with these customers.

These services Austin Food Tech offers cater to customers' vital needs. So what if they have nothing to do with Carol's previous corporate expertise or her favorite activities? She knows that to succeed, she must listen to customers instead of pitching her services.

Carol's knowledge of chemistry and food interactions paid off again shortly after Austin Food Tech opened. When the commercial food industry was hit with a tomato paste shortage, it was a big problem for everyone from pizza producers to Mexican food makers. They had to figure out how to make their products without tomatoes if they were to meet production schedules. Tomatoes are practically Hunt Wesson's middle name, so Carol knows a great deal about how people perceive tomatoes in a recipe: the right balance of acid, sweetness, salt, red color, and pulpy texture. She could tell these companies how to make their foods without tomato—a solution for all but those bound by government regulations to contain a specified amount of the real McCoy.

Many food companies also rent their facilities to contract food manufacturers, so Carol often asks to tour the kitchens of potential clients in case her existing clients need places to lease. While she's touring, Carol sets her antennae for problems the companies have with their own products.

"You learn to listen, to ask about problems that Austin Food Tech services will solve. It doesn't come off like a sales call," she says. "I've never had a food company say it doesn't want to talk to me. And, eventually, it will send business my way."

**TIPS...**

**53.** Counting a portion of your inventory each day is a more effective means of tracking your stock than a once-a-year tally.

**54.** Just because you're not yet one of the most successful business owners in America doesn't mean you shouldn't act as professional as one.

**55.** As a new business, your role is, in part, to shake up the status quo.

**56.** Set your sights on goals of specific dates and amounts. You'll go as far as your aim.

**57.** Learn something new each day about running and growing a successful business.

**58.** Always act as if your best possible customer is about to walk through the door.

**59.** Forget what you want. Figure out what someone will pay you to do.

**60.** Love your business dream. Sacrifice for it. Always move forward.

**61.** If that big corporate customer says no, keep knocking on the door.

**62.** Even when you're desperate, check the credit of potential customers.

**63.** Always establish a backup plan for leadership with open communication and cross training.

**64.** Allow technology instead of the costly expansion of overhead to build your company.

**65.** If you can't find suppliers, take it as an opportunity for business growth you hadn't anticipated.

**66.** Leave your customers begging for more, but not so loudly that you open the doors for competitors to satisfy those unmet desires.

**67.** Hire the management help you need to manage growth without shortages or burnout.

**68.** Investigate franchisers before you invest.

**69.** If you listen, your customers' requests will guide your business growth.

# PART 5

# HELPING HAND(S)

## ...

**E**very new business owner needs help. Even the one-person home-based operation can accomplish more at greater speed and with less hassle with assistance. Others have been where you are now. You'll be astounded how helpful they are willing to be if you let them know you need and value their advice.

You really know your business is on its way when you start tapping the help of outside experts. (Just remember, you own the place; don't abdicate that role to any expert.) However, the real challenge begins when you hire help. Communication is key when you take on the role of employer along with business owner. You must relate your needs and expectations to job applicants as well as employees. They will never do the job right if you don't explain it first. Employees who know the rules of the game are likely to follow them. Those who are rewarded for meeting your goals are likely to exceed them.

But it all begins with you. You define the job descriptions. You set the rules. You establish the goals. You create the rewards. The catch is that new business owners, especially those who chafed at the rules in former corporate jobs, really hate to create the needed structure.

# 70. DELEGATE TO GROW

Learn to delegate authority over routine
jobs so you can spend more time
growing the business.

■ ■ ■

As a child, Richard Yobs sold eggs door to door with his father.

"Never work for anyone else if you can help it," the senior Yobs advised during their travels.

That advice planted a seed in Richard's mind that took root when he accepted a job as manager of a paint store when he was in his early 20s.

"From the day I went into that job, I thought I could own my own store someday if things went right," Richard says.

His boss was rarely at the store, so Richard learned every aspect of paint retailing "except signing the paychecks." It was invaluable experience.

"Too many people go into business without taking the time to learn how first," he says.

After five years of managing and learning on the job, Richard opened Painten Place in Denville, New Jersey, in 1971. The retail paint and wall covering store has hundreds of commercial accounts as well has individual customers. Richard supplies expertise and information even professional painters don't have.

In the beginning, Richard did it all. "I needed to learn how to delegate authority, not just go through the motions," Richard says. "You must delegate day-to-day jobs, so you can spend more time growing your business, buying better, and networking."

The cost to a business is monumental, sometimes fatal, if the entrepreneur spends too much time on routine tasks that anyone can do and never gets around to the strategic planning and high-level work that only the owner can do.

"Oh, I'd give someone the keys and let him open or close, but I never gave anyone the authority to make a decision so I could get out to make important sales calls," Richard says. "Then, as soon as I left, the store would get busy, and I'd have to run back and make decisions."

A business owner has only so much time. Richard could spend all his time in the store doing a $6-an-hour clerk's job, or he could hire someone else to do that job and devote his time to going out to customers' locations and selling.

"On the road, I'm worth $1,000 an hour," he says.

Few entrepreneurs know instinctively how to delegate. Fewer yet want to. They try to do everything, usually for one of two reasons. They think they can't afford help, or they think no one can do the job as well as they can.

"If you allow people to make decisions, they will," Richard says. "They are going to make mistakes because we all do, but then they learn and do better the next time."

Getting over his own do-it-all syndrome took extreme self-discipline, Richard says. First, he had to hire and train people to work in the store and service the customers the way he wanted it done.

"Then I had to say, 'Bye, I'm going out on the road; you'll have to do it without me,'" he says. "It took a couple of years for me to get comfortable leaving."

Now Painten Place has two employees whom Richard trusts with the whole operation. The other five he can count on to fill in for brief periods or in specific jobs.

"Delegation is the only way a company can grow" Richard says. "The business gets too big for the owner to do it all."

# 71. YA GOTTA ASK

So many people are willing to help the new
business owner, but an unwillingness to ask
for help forces the entrepreneur to
learn everything the hard way.

■ ■ ■

You name it, Bernard "Barney" Hale Zick has probably negotiated, syndicated, or marketed it. After earning his MBA in investment, he worked on Wall Street, then marketed insurance, oil drilling, real estate, and mutual fund investments. He has run everything from truck stops to computer software companies.

In 1973, Barney applied all this experience to launching Zick Communications, Inc., a Kingwood, Texas, firm that helps companies develop their business-to-business marketing and sales strategies. He also teaches investment seminars.

"I had an MBA and lots of 'smarts,' but I was unwilling to ask for help," Barney says. "I paid dearly for the lessons I learned the hard way. It would have been an easier path if I would have learned to ask for help earlier."

Barney attributes this reluctance to youthful ignorance. "I felt I had to know everything," he says. "You don't. But you do need to know what you don't know and gather people around you who can fill in these gaps."

However, many other inexperienced entrepreneurs of all ages suffer from this same reluctance. They don't ask, so they don't receive. And it's so unnecessary to reinvent the wheel this way, Barney says. "People enjoy sharing advice; they consider it a compliment, an ego boost."

Advisers abound in the business world. The best places to start looking for these experts is trade associations, chambers of commerce, and industry publications. Anyone who has ever written a business or marketing plan knows the value of demographic and industry information these groups supply. They are reservoirs of human capital as well.

Within business groups, look for people who have similar jobs in related companies. Novices often believe that competitors won't share information, and in some industries, this is true. However, it's amazing what people will tell you if you are genuinely interested, willing to accept advice, and do as much background preparation as possible before asking questions. Nothing ends an advisory relationship faster than failure to heed the counsel, however.

Barney doesn't just join trade associations: he becomes actively involved. He also networks extensively with other professional trainers and consultants.

"I frequently ask experts what they think," he says. "And in consulting, speaking, and writing on my topics, I ask questions, questions, questions."

Barney never had a mentor.

What's a mentor? In Greek mythology, Mentor was the loyal friend and adviser of Odysseus, king of Ithaca and a Greek leader in the Trojan War. In the 20th century, the name has become synonymous with the friendly, experienced executive who gives a younger colleague a boost up the business ladder.

Mentors usually are associated with large corporations, but the mentoring process works equally well among small-business owners. Venture clubs and executive forums usually have formal procedures for matching bright young entrepreneurs with experienced business owners. Many college business departments and alumni associations also have established mentoring programs.

Today, Barney finds himself more often the mentor than the student.

"After having success and my share of disappointments," he says, "I now give advice to others so they can get more of what they want out of life in less time."

# 72. THE GAME OF SEEK AND KEEP

### It is difficult for small businesses to find and keep production workers.

■ ■ ■

**A**nne Grimes, a one-time deli manager for a large supermarket, owned a small bake shop in Ayden, North Carolina. Customers often asked for dumplings to put in their chicken recipes, but Anne always told them she didn't make dumplings—until one persistent customer wore her down.

Anne dumped some ingredients into a mixer, rolled out the dough, and froze four boxes of dumplings. The customer was so delighted with the product that word spread that Anne made the most delicious dumplings, convenient because they were frozen.

Anne and her husband, Bryan, bought a pastry-making machine and converted their home carport into a dumpling factory in 1981. They called their side venture Harvest Time Foods. Sales exploded so rapidly, first to grocery stores and then to warehouses that supplied grocery chains, that Anne closed the bakery and Bryan quit his job as manager of a hospital parking lot. Their son, Bryan III, was recruited to help with distribution.

Within a year, the Grimeses moved Harvest Time Foods into a commercial building, and three years later, they bought a larger building. When they moved again, they converted the former factory into a youth center and donated it to a church.

Despite its success, the company has always had difficulty hiring and keeping enough production workers. These jobs do not demand a high level of education, but require people who understand the importance of production quotas and quality products.

"Although no training is needed for our production jobs, we prefer high school graduates with good work ethics," Anne says.

The Grimeses are not alone. Many fast-growing start-up businesses have difficulty finding workers. Then, after the expense of training new hires, the companies have difficulty keeping them. Small businesses usually are at a disadvantage when it comes to pay rates, fringe benefits, and opportunities for advancement within the company. Companies like Harvest Time Foods, trying to fill entry-level jobs, struggle more. In rural areas and times of low unemployment, the problem is worse.

Anne thinks internship and apprenticeship programs at local schools and colleges might have helped Harvest Time Foods solve its problem. The company could have worked with the schools in its area to create a combination of classroom education and on-the-job experience. Other companies offer employees cash rewards for helping recruit new employees. Still others send recruiters to trade shows, community fairs, and even parks on sunny weekend afternoons. Harvest Time Foods resorted to mechanical help.

"We have elected to automate every area of our production facility as funds become available," Anne says.

Originally, Harvest Time Foods' workers mixed, rolled, and cut pastry dough into dumplings. They then hand-packed the completed product and wrapped the boxes. The Grimeses have since found machinery to do all that work, including layering the dumplings in boxes without damaging them.

Over a three-year period, the company's staffing needs declined from 55 jobs to 8 with triple the production capacity. However, Harvest Time Foods did not lay off workers. Because the automation process was accomplished over several years, the company brought in temporary workers whenever permanent employees left. Today, retailers and distributors in 20 states buy the frozen dumplings. Bryan III became company president in 1996.

"By reducing our workforce by automation, we can offer higher wages to the workers we keep," says Anne, who is still company secretary/treasurer and head of sales development.

# 73.

## HIRE THE BEST

Many business start-ups try to save money
by hiring cheap labor. It pays to hire
the best quality personnel.

■ ■ ■

**S**cott Sorensen had just graduated from college when he stepped in to save the family moving company in 1977. His mother had kept Sorensen Moving & Storage afloat since his father's death, but Melbourne, Florida, was in a prolonged recession that threatened to sink the agent for Allied Van Lines.

"Many times, because of budgetary constraints, new business owners—and owners of established businesses, for that matter—try to get by hiring cheap," Scott says. "I have learned from experience that it pays to hire the best people you can because your business is only as good as the team members associated with you."

Scott has learned to define the overall team his company needs, to carefully craft job descriptions for the individuals who make up that team, and to clarify some intangibles that pull the two together. Taking time to clarify these work goals helps business owners know what they're looking for when hiring. It also attracts the right employees.

Scott started with the big picture: "The best team is one that can work together to meet individual objectives and company goals at the same time," he says. To build that team, it helps to develop objective, job-related selection criteria. If the worker must be able to type, don't hire someone who can't. If the job requires selling experience, don't hire someone who has none.

In his search for the best managers, Scott often recruits from other industries. For the best sales and marketing people, he recruits from competitors. He also looks for qualifications not found on any resume.

"I look for attitude; people who can be good team players within the organization; for good values away from work; and for people who can do more than just the jobs they're being hired for," he explains.

Scott wants people with multiple work capabilities because he believes in hiring from within. He also wants workers eager for greater responsibilities. In fact, he employs at least 15 managers who worked their way up through the company. One former employee was so eager for greater responsibility, however, that he left to start his own moving company in another market.

Scott acknowledges that his hires aren't always perfect.

"We'd like to hire all 9s and 10s, of course, but sometimes a 7 or 8 is the best we can find," he says. "They're outstanding in one area, but weak in another. So we have to match their strengths with our jobs."

That's a juggling act that many inexperienced business owners fail to appreciate.

Scott became good enough at finding and keeping the right staffing combination that he was able to expand beyond residential and business moves into additional services, such as transporting high-tech equipment. He also opened a separate Allied Van Lines franchise in Orlando, Florida, in 1994, using managers from the Melbourne company to run it. He did the same in opening a self-storage company.

"I always hope to promote from within," he says. "The higher caliber the personnel you have on your team, the more you put yourself in a position to be successful."

# 74. YOU CAN'T ASK THAT!

New employers must learn to hire
the right employees without asking
legally prohibited questions.

■ ■ ■

**N**ancy Friedman was so angered by the rude way her insurance broker's employees treated her on the phone that she cancelled all her policies. The stunned broker asked Nancy to come in and talk with his employees about proper phone etiquette. She certainly was familiar with the topic. She handled customer relations for her husband's business, Weatherline, Inc., a telephone weather report service in St. Louis, Missouri.

That presentation in 1982 was the start of Telephone Doctor, a company that trains businesspeople worldwide in proper phone manners through seminars and videotapes.

However, if Telephone Doctor is going to be credible, employees must practice what Nancy preaches.

"It's so hard to hire the right people because there are so many questions employers can't ask job applicants," Nancy says.

Many questions once common in a job interview have been made illegal by federal and state laws prohibiting job discrimination based on ethnicity, sex, age, religion or disability. Even some questions job interviewers used to ask to put applicants at ease, such as do you have children or are you married, are off limits.

For example, you can't ask job applicants whether they have diseases that aren't job related. You can't question whether they have ever been arrested. (You can, however, determine whether they have ever been convicted of a felony.) You can't ask whether they belong to certain clubs (which might indicate religion or ethnicity) or even whether they are male or female.

The key to avoiding legal problems is to focus the interview on job requirements and company policies. For instance, you can describe the work that is part of a job and ask whether the applicant can do it. If it's a warehouse job, can the applicant lift 50-pound boxes? If it's a delivery job, does the applicant have a valid driver's license, and can he drive 200 miles a day, five days a week? A disabled person might be able to do a job with some accommodation that you are required to provide. For example, a person may be a whiz-bang typist, but need wheelchair access to the building.

But just as significant as avoiding illegal questions is finding the right questions to weed out applicants poorly suited for particular jobs. The last thing Telephone Doctor needs is someone who is rude on the phone, for example.

"I need people who can think on their feet. They must be knowledgeable, friendly," Nancy says. "We give applicants a simple quiz. What newspapers do you read? Who is the vice president of the United States? Questions like that. I won't hire someone who doesn't know the vice president."

Each employer should carefully craft some questions that get to the heart of the job being filled. For example, to assess leadership skills, you might ask how the applicant would discipline an errant worker. However, word it in such a way that you can determine whether the applicant has any experience. Say, for instance, "Tell me about a time when you had to discipline an employee." Or describe a situation that your workers really encounter in their jobs, and ask the applicant to role-play a solution.

Don't rely on interviews alone, however. Too many people have taken seminars in how to ace a job interview. Always check references and, if appropriate, give a skills test.

Nancy's employees are friendly, helpful, and—you hear in their voices— smiling. They never say, "I don't know" without adding "but I'll find out for you." All of these are skills that Nancy teaches employees at other corporations, so, naturally, they're part of the job description at Telephone Doctor.

# 75. COMPLEMENT YOURSELF

Hire people with skills different than yours that
supply needed expertise in running a business.

■ ■ ■

**P**am Lontos was so good at selling radio advertising for her broadcast employer that her boss wanted to make her the general manager of one of the company's radio stations. But Pam knew her skills and interests lay in selling and training others to sell, not in doing budgets and paperwork. So, in 1981, Pam started Lontos Sales & Motivation, a consulting, training, and seminar firm in Dallas, Texas. It is now headquartered in Orlando, Florida.

"I would hire people just like myself," says Pam, an effervescent personality who once had her own television program. "I have since found that other business owners tend to do the same thing. Creative people hire creative people.

"So I had all creative people in my office, and no one balanced the checkbook for two months. The bills didn't get paid."

Pam's office was fun and full of energy, with everyone chatting with each other all the time, but the work wasn't getting done. She also hired more people than she needed. She had someone to type articles, another to answer the phones, several to sell, a supervisor to run the office, even someone to come in and water the plants.

"My expenses were ridiculous," Pam says. "Clients don't come to me, I go to them. There was no reason to have that many people."

She reduced her staff to three.

"Plus, I'm always on the road," Pam adds, "so I gave my plants away and cancelled that service."

Then Pam started hiring people strong in the areas in which she is weak or has no interest.

"It's almost like hiring your opposite," she says.

Pam is more comfortable talking than writing, so she speaks her letters, speeches, and other material into a tape recorder and has a hired assistant transcribe and polish the work in writing.

"When hiring, I ask for people who can type," she says. "My first typist couldn't spell. A lot of people don't check that."

When Pam needed an outside accounting firm, she asked a friend she trusted for a referral. That friend recommended someone in another state, but the long-distance relationship works well with faxes and telephones, Pam says. She pays a monthly retainer to the firm, which does all her bookkeeping.

"I find a reasonably priced accountant is worth it," she says. "He saves you on taxes, and you have no problem if audited."

Pam has an outside attorney she trusts, also in another state, whom she pays an hourly rate rather than a retainer to review every contract. The advances in technology have made these business relationships possible, she says.

Eventually, Pam's husband, Rick, a former geophysicist with a head for business, came aboard to handle the business side of the company, leaving Pam free to concentrate on sales, consulting, and training. But Pam never delegates the part of her business that is her strength and she loves most—the training—even though it means she is on the road ten days a month.

"I've seen too many people get so involved in the paperwork of the business that they stop doing something they love and then lose the passion, the drive that makes them good at what they do," she explains.

The problem with running such a lean company is the absence of "atta boys," Pam says.

"You don't have someone looking over your shoulder criticizing you, but you also don't have someone patting you on the back," she says. "The entrepreneur has to be self-motivated."

# 76.
## WIN-WIN PAY STRUCTURES

Don't give away the store when establishing
a pay structure for employees.

■ ■ ■

**W**hen Paula and Jim Brown started JB Chemical Co. in the garage of their Las Vegas, Nevada, home, they wanted to give as much as possible to their employees. Jim had been in sales and knew how important the sales staff would be to establishing JB Chemical's 800 environmentally safe cleaning products in the local market. The company sells mostly in bulk to large industrial users.

The Browns established a pay structure that gave their sales staff a salary plus a commission that was a high percentage of gross profit. The rate was the same for every salesperson, regardless of production. The Browns also allowed the salespeople some flexibility in the price they charged, which could save a sale if a salesperson had to meet a competitor's price or give the salesperson more income if he could charge more and still beat the competition. They found out later that competitors paid substantially lower commission rates.

As the industry became increasingly competitive, JB Chemical was at a price disadvantage, and altering the commission structure was extremely difficult, Paula says. However, the company had to change the way it paid its sales force or lose money.

Payroll is often the largest expense a company has. While generous salaries can help attract good employees, the company must be able to afford them. The pay structure must create a win-win situation that is most effective in boosting sales and profitability.

"New business owners should do their due diligence to find out how other companies are paying their workers," Paula says. "The commission structure is the oldest form of salary compensation, so you can certainly find out information from other business owners."

If local competitors won't disclose such information, talk with business owners in other industries or with owners of similar companies in other markets that don't compete with yours, Paula suggests.

"Now with the Internet, I would search online for companies by SIC code and write letters to 20 of them, asking how they pay their salespeople," she says.

JB Chemical finally changed its pricing schedule to customers and its commission schedule to the sales staff. Customers now get a price break for buying larger volume, which helps boost sales without hurting profit margins.

The company also established sales quotas. Salespeople who meet their quotas get a percentage of gross profits that is lower than the company used to pay, but higher than the industry standard. Those who fail to meet their sales quotas get lower percentages. Those who exceed their quotas get a higher percentages.

"Of course, this incentive selling went over like a lead balloon," Paula says. She proposed an alternative structure, which employees liked even less. Significantly, though, no one quit. Following the new structure, "Some people earned a lower commission because they didn't make quota," she says, "and two took it as a challenge and earned the higher commission rate."

As a new business owner, you are better off if you figure out these compensation issues early in your company's life. To save the company's profitability later, you risk losing or alienating your employees, who must represent you to customers. Once you tell people the work they are doing is worth a certain amount of money, they don't want to do it for less, even if that's the going wage every other company in your industry pays. When a company struggles financially, the owner might win employees over by asking them to help decide how best to save the company. Does everyone sacrifice a little pay? Can jobs be eliminated without making the matter worse?

Paula was smart to create a plan that could actually give salespeople a pay raise and benefit the company, too. Now *that's* a real win-win pay structure.

# 77.     IT'S POLICY

A new business should have written policies
and procedures from the beginning.

■ ■ ■

After working as a claims supervisor for an insurance company, Steve
Salem joined his father's temporary employment agency, Rudy Salem
Staffing Services, in Sioux City, Iowa, in 1987.

Rudy ran the business informally, without written policies and procedures. That approach made the company vulnerable to employees who
overstepped their bounds, wanted more vacation than they had earned, or
did their jobs poorly, says Steve, who bought out his father in 1991.

Many small-business owners actively resist writing policies and procedures. They hated them when they worked in big corporations, and by
golly, they're not going to be hog-tied by them in their own companies.
Others have been warned by attorneys that written policies will only get
them into trouble.

Poorly written policies certainly can cause trouble, but lack of any written policies or procedures can cause more trouble, both legal and organizational. Even the smallest employer has the legal responsibility not to
discriminate and not to tolerate sexual harassment. Companies with as few
as 15 employees must abide by the Americans with Disabilities Act in hiring. You don't waive your obligation if you avoid putting these rules in
writing; you merely leave supervisors uninformed of their duties.

The most significant benefit of rules and procedures is that they ensure
everyone has the same vision and is moving in the same direction. If you,
as owner, don't establish the vision and direction, your workers will make
up their own.

Companies flounder without procedural roadmaps. And in an increasingly litigious society, they can sink under the weight of lawsuits for discrimination, sexual harassment, and wrongful termination. Sixty percent of
U.S. employers have been defendants in employment practices lawsuits in
the 1990s alone.

Many of these problems arise because employees misunderstand what they are told or believe they have been treated unfairly. The employee handbook, for example, should specify employee benefits.

"Some people won't even take the vacations to which they're entitled," Steve says. "Others take all their vacation and want more. You end up with divisiveness between the martyrs and the abusers."

Companies need to write their policies clearly, in plain English, and enforce them uniformly. And the sooner companies establish these formal procedures and policies, the better.

"We've found it difficult to change our informal culture despite the need to do so. It's better to start out the way you eventually hope to end up," Steve concludes.

When writing employee policies, business owners must carefully avoid any potentially discriminatory language. Also, they should make sure they can live with any policies they write and follow what they have written. For example, let's say you have a company policy that any employee caught stealing will be fired. You catch Joe with his hand in the till, but you let him off with a warning because he's a hard worker. If you catch another employee stealing and fire him, he can claim a breach of good faith and fair dealing because you treated Joe differently.

Policies should avoid any wording that restricts an owner's discretion in dealing with issues. And if policies contain lists—for example, causes of termination—those lists should be labeled as examples, not all-inclusive inventories.

Policies also should include consequences for violation, such as progressive discipline leading to dismissal for continued poor work performance. However, the focus must be on employee behavior on the job. Company policy can't specify termination for a worker who drinks in his spare time if the drinking doesn't affect his job performance.

If you have trouble defining your own policies and procedures, you might consider hiring consultants, as Steve did, to help put your company on a more formal track. Although the bulk of Salem Staffing's business had been in finding temporary workers for client companies, consultants helped Steve expand the company's base to permanent job placement, executive searches, and on-the-job safety consulting. Steve has involved employees in the transition, establishing guidelines for fringe benefits.

"We're moving toward a cafeteria plan of benefits," he says. "I don't have to decide which benefits are important. My staff will pick for themselves."

# 78. GET A SECOND OPINION

Enlist the help of professional advisers,
but always balance their advice with
your own knowledge and the
recommendations of others.

■ ■ ■

Inventing is in Bill Bresnahan's bloodline; his great-great-uncle, Roger, a former major league baseball player, invented the batting helmet and catcher's shin guards. After Bill was wounded and retired as a police officer, he turned to his creative side.

Bill holds 18 patents and has not only invented, but brought to market—through his West Chester, Pennsylvania, company, RVI II—cardboard folding binoculars, a windshield wiper blade sharpener, a combination pizza cutter and lid support, and a key ring puzzle.

Such efforts require professional help, but a business owner always should get a second opinion, Bill says. In fact, if you don't balance professional advice with personal research, it could cost you a great deal of time and money. For example, without Bill's knowledge, a patent agent changed some of the claims on a patent application, which reduced its profit potential. Another attorney wrote a template for a nondisclosure agreement that later proved to be ineffective.

"You have to rely on the pros," Bill says, "but you don't have to trust them. I take what they tell me, and then I get other bids, other suggestions."

Bill taught himself about the patent process by doing research and asking questions at the U.S. Patent and Trademark Office in Washington, D.C. Public libraries throughout the country also provide a great deal of information, plus they have computer equipment to allow inventors to do their own patent searches. And the Internet has become a cornucopia of patent information.

Many things cannot be patented, such as abstract ideas that cannot be reduced to tangible forms or products that cannot produce the claimed result. For those inventions that can be patented, the patents are not automatic; the process can take two years. To begin, an inventor must file an application with the U.S. Patent and Trade Office that follows the expected conventions and clearly explains, in words and drawings, why the invention deserves a patent, how to make the invention, and why it's different from previous creations.

As the number of patents has grown, this process has become increasingly complex and difficult to maneuver without help. That's why professionals can make healthy livings off novice inventors. Some applications go back and forth many times between the inventors and the government patent examiners. If an inventor can overcome an examiner's objections, a patent is approved. By law, independent inventors pay half the fee that large companies do to have patents issued. They must pay additional fees to keep the patents alive in future years.

Still, a patent won't sell your invention. Bill also taught himself to market his products by writing press releases and winning contests, including the 1989 Galilean Award from the Smithsonian Institution for the most innovative telescope. He even submitted one of his inventions to the Guinness Book of World Records as the world's smallest folding cardboard binoculars.

The binoculars have been Bill's biggest hit. They were licensed by the Olympic committees for 1988, 1996, 1998, and 2000. They also have licenses with the National Hockey League, 1998 Malaysian Commonwealth Games, and 1999 Pan–American Games. They were featured on boxes of Kellogg's Frosted Flakes in a joint promotion with the YMCA in Canada, and they have been sold for $5 to $10 in Wal-mart and Sears. More than a million of the binoculars have been sold or given away as premiums.

"Everyone thinks the work I do is a piece of cake," Bill says. "Yeah, if you don't mind spending 12 years making [something]. Wisdom comes with experience."

# 79.

## SIDE ONE:
## GET A PARTNER

Don't try to do everything alone.
A partner is an invaluable ally.

■ ■ ■

**W**hile working in sales for computer companies, Patty Musich never could find all the demographic information she wanted about her market. It was scattered among too many government agencies and private organizations. Her research confirmed that other companies had similar frustrations.

In 1985, Patty started Focus Publications to publish an annual directory of statistics, demographics, and information about the cities in Orange County, California. She began with $20,000 in personal savings and investments from business friends, but she was continually short of help and money.

"I should have had a partner and not tried to do it all alone," Patty says. "A partner could bring money, experience, and ideas, as well as share the workload. A partnership definitely could have increased my success with less effort."

Long work days and self-discipline were the only things that saved Focus Publications in the early years. Patty was always looking for a financial partner, but resisted bringing in a business partner. In 1992, she hired a business acquaintance, Dan Harrison, to develop a program to sell advertising in her magazine-like publication.

"Dan brought to the table the advertising experience I lacked," Patty says. "I had developed tunnel vision because I was wearing so many hats as a sole proprietor."

Dan also brought a big-picture view to Focus Publications that enabled the company to start publishing a San Diego edition. Because the pair worked so well together, with complementary skills, matching personalities, and shared vision for the company, Patty asked Dan to become a partner.

"He resisted at first because this was my baby," Patty says. "He didn't think he had the personal attachment that I had; he was working on other projects."

Finally, however, in 1994, Dan agreed to become a partner in Focus Publications. Together, Patty and Dan expanded the publication into other regions.

"It was good to have worked together before forming the partnership," Patty says. "We got to experience each other's work habits and styles before we formalized it."

Their relationship was so good that Patty and Dan married in 1996.

Although most partners never tie the marital knot, a business partnership is a lot like a marriage. The partners commit themselves as well as their money—they had better be compatible. But partnerships that work best bring together people with separate strengths. Dan brought advertising and management experience that Patty knew was necessary for company growth. And Dan didn't try to run the whole show.

A partnership should have a written agreement that spells out every partner's contributions and responsibilities. Some partners bring only money to the relationship. Although Patty had looked for that type of partner initially, the approach has problems, she says, because financial partners usually lack the emotional commitment a small company needs.

Often, partners contribute a special talent, a type of experience, or contacts beneficial to the company. Those contributions should have worth in the agreement just as money does because they help determine the delegation of management duties. A former accountant becomes the company's chief financial officer. A one-time manager takes over as chief executive officer. A computer whiz is perfect as technology vice president.

A partnership often changes a company's direction. In 1997, Patty and Dan linked Focus Publications with Homeseekers.Com, an Internet real estate guide. Focus Publications now provides demographic information for all strong real estate markets nationwide, and it partners with economic development agencies that want demographic publications for their communities.

# *80.*   FLIP SIDE: FORGET A PARTNER

A partnership can be an absolute disaster
if the parties ignore the need for
a written agreement.

■ ■ ■

**R**oy Robbins had the entrepreneurial itch. He was tired of his job as senior process engineer at a huge aerospace company and had developed a five-year plan to leave corporate America to start a bookstore. Roy had collected books for 15 years and worked part time in bookstores to learn the business. When his employer offered a voluntary buyout in 1992, he grabbed it.

Roy started Badmoon Books, a mail-order and Internet bookseller specializing in collectible editions of horror stories and mysteries. Although the business was based in his Anaheim, California, home, he hosted author book signings at standard bookstores owned by friends.

A friend from the aerospace company also was interested in book retailing and had the cash and expertise to team up on a regular store, so Roy jumped into the partnership. Never again, he says. "That partnership was a major mistake."

Friendship isn't enough to sustain a partnership. In fact, partnerships have been known to kill life-long friendships. After their bookstore faltered and finally closed, Roy and his ex-partner weren't enemies, but they never talked.

"It's very hard to make a partnership work, anyway," Roy says, "and when people have different goals and values, they will clash."

Successful partnerships need written agreements from the beginning. Unsuccessful partnerships need them even more. A typical partnership agreement should state a specific purpose for the business, each partner's tangible (money, property, equipment, patents) and intangible (services, special skills, contacts) contributions, and each partner's percentage of the business in return for those contributions. Such agreements can be structured so one partner owns a bigger share than the others do. The agreement should also specify each partner's management responsibilities and whether he or she can have outside business activities. Roy, for example, continued his mail-order business.

Perhaps most important, the agreement should specify how partners can end their arrangement. Like partners in marriage, partners in business don't like to talk about divorce ahead of time, but these decisions can be made more fairly up front, uncolored by the rancor that can build through the experience. If one partner dies or wants out, the remaining partners should have the opportunity to buy his or her share. Some successful, long-time partnerships run into trouble when one partner dies and his heirs, who have never been involved before, insist on joining the business. The agreement also should determine how a departing partner's share would be valued and paid.

Often, partnerships end bitterly; some issues just cannot be resolved. A written partnership agreement can save the partners the time and expense of a lawsuit by spelling out a means for resolving disputes, usually arbitration or mediation. Even if partners are relatives or best friends, they should have separate attorneys review the agreement before signing.

Roy and his partner did not achieve the complementary working relationship that Patty and Dan did at Focus Communications (Profile 79). Roy attributes much of their differences to a personality clash. He is much happier now running Badmoon Books by himself—even if it means starting work at 5:00 AM to respond to e-mail from his European customers or working three days straight when he has to publish a new catalog. But, then, he has no hassles if he wants to go to one of his son's events.

"You have to be driven to be a small-business owner," Roy says. "I work harder now than I ever did at my corporate job. Yet I'm never as tired as I used to be there."

# 81.   TURN PRO

If you don't have a professional management
team from the start, the transition from
mom-and-pop business to professionally
run company is hard.

■ ■ ■

**A**fter graduating from college, Casey Nickerson raced sailboats in the Caribbean. Three years later in 1976, he wanted to find a use for his industrial engineering degree, so he started Nickerson Assembly Co. in Tilton, New Hampshire. The one-employee company manufactured electronic wiring for printed circuit boards and custom-assembled boards for original equipment manufacturers.

Casey ran Nickerson Assembly like a mom-and-pop operation for years—a practice that created enormous stress for Casey and limited company growth. A one-person leadership style may work when a company is small, Casey says, "but when you start doing million-dollar contracts, your customers are looking at the expertise you have doing the work. I should have had a more professional management team in the beginning."

Many entrepreneurs cannot let go of all the responsibility, even if they realize their companies cannot survive and grow without it. And if they try to let go, the transition is not that easy to achieve, Casey says. In 1994, Casey made his own decision to create a professional management team at Nickerson Assembly. The long delay made the transformation even more arduous, he admits.

A business owner should begin by analyzing carefully the work his company does, how it gets done, and what his own core competencies are. This study shouldn't be undertaken quickly or carelessly. Well-defined descriptions further the process that is half intended to help the entrepreneur let go and half intended to guide the search for persons whose skills and personalities match the company's needs. When the business owner has completed his analysis, he should keep the core responsibilities and hand off the remainder of the work to experts who know best how to do it. Each configuration varies, depending on the personalities of the individual company and owner.

In the management structure Casey developed, he saw himself providing oversight of seven managers in charge of quality, production, accounting, engineering, human resources, materials, and sales.

"The last two are key," Casey says. "Manufacturers have to have those two things under control, or else big problems come their way."

However, filling the management positions with the best people was slow and difficult, Casey says. "I had to understand the different basic personalities to better match jobs with the people. People want to do well, but the company must be able to put them in the places where they can excel."

Even with that scrutiny, the process didn't flow effortlessly. Casey had 20 different people in his seven key management positions before he thought he had the right combination.

"You can't just find one person and say that will work," he says. "You have to dig and dig. You have to bring in really talented people."

Many companies don't survive the transition to professional management team, partly because of the additional expense it puts on the company, Casey says. "Customers don't want to pay more, but your prices have to go up. We did a lot of cost analysis to understand which jobs were hurting us financially. Then we raised prices very tenderly."

The two-year transition to the new management structure paid enormous benefits, Casey says. "I can actually feel the orders going through the roof. Before, we didn't have controls in place to handle them. Now we can accept more large contracts."

# 82. TAKE CARE OF THE CHILD

Home-based business owners must
eliminate the crying baby, barking dog,
and friendly neighbor, all of whom steal
professionalism and concentration.

■ ■ ■

In 1988, Toni Korby started Antonia Korby Design, Inc., making curtains and bedspreads in her Centreville, Virginia home, so she could be with her children, who were one and three years old at the time. A third baby was born two years later.

"The whole purpose of working out of the home was to take care of my kids," Toni says, "but if I were to do it again, I would have paid more attention to childcare sooner."

Thousands of women and men start home-based businesses for lifestyle reasons such as care of small children or elderly parents. They often discover that home life and business are not completely compatible. Unless the entrepreneur deals honestly with these incompatibilities, one or the other—perhaps both—will suffer.

Toni had to strike a balance between work time and childcare time.

"I tried all kinds of arrangements," she says. "I took my daughter to a woman's house. Preschool allowed my children to stay through lunch, so I got a block of four hours to work in the mornings every other day."

One summer, Toni hired a woman to watch the children in her home, but "that didn't work out well," she says. "I could still hear the kids. It was very distracting."

Most clients these days don't care where their suppliers are based. They will take your business as seriously as you do, regardless of where it is headquartered. Clients merely ask that the work be done correctly and on time. Toni never hid that she worked from home, as home-based business owners used to do in past decades.

Two factors are at work on the home-based enterprise, however. One is the appearance of professionalism. There are no barking dogs or crying babies in high-rise offices. The other is the owner's ability to work under chaotic conditions. Home often is more hectic than a corporate office.

Some huge enterprises had humble home-based beginnings. Milton Hershey started making candy in his kitchen. Steve Jobs and Stephen Wozniak made the first Apple computer in Jobs' garage. Your enterprise could grow to be as big as theirs if you treat it seriously.

Home-based business owners usually blow their credibility by failing to separate personal life and business. They don't get the licenses or fictitious business names to form their businesses legally. They don't keep regular business hours. They don't have separate business telephone lines that they answer professionally. And the notion of a home-based business solving childcare problems is a myth. Entrepreneur parents find themselves making business calls during naptime, using day care centers to grab some uninterrupted work hours, and calling on neighbors or babysitters when a business crisis arises.

In some areas, home-business owners form informal alliances or formal clubs to share childcare duties. Perhaps one parent takes the children on Monday and Wednesday mornings and the other takes them Tuesday and Thursday afternoons, freeing up uninterrupted time for appointments or production without worries of child safety. If anything, the entrepreneur parent must work faster and be more organized than other business owners.

"I call it the juggle-juggle act," says Toni, who has expanded her business to supplying artwork, window blinds, and other home furnishings. "I've gotten better at time management in recent years. I plan my schedule to drop something off at one client's place on the way to another appointment, for example."

It also helps that her children are now school age.

# 83. LINK WITH OTHERS

### Strategic partnerships will help
### finance a start-up.

■  ■  ■

**W**hen single mother Diana Todaro didn't want her son to eat a lot of sugary, high-fat junk food, she created her own cookies from whole grains, nuts, and dried fruits. She figured that moms everywhere probably were looking for wholesome snacks made without preservatives or artificial flavors, so in 1990, she used her recipes to launch Diana's California Cookies in Laguna Hills, California.

Diana's Cookies wasn't Nabisco. She financed the start-up out of her own pocket. She handled the sales and marketing herself. One of her brothers was company attorney. Another brother was financial adviser.

Diana sold more than a million cookies in her first three months in business, but without the help of unrelated companies, Diana's Cookies never would have gotten off the ground.

The first alliance Diana made was with a contract bakery. This arrangement saved her company the expense of building or buying its own factory and warehouse.

After trial runs in several U.S. supermarket chains, Diana started her own distribution through toll-free phone service and mail order. She also started selling her cookies under the labels of other cookie companies—more important alliances to help Diana's Cookies grow.

A one-time travel agent who had visited 25 foreign countries, Diana made international expansion a part of her company's growth plan from the start.

To better understand her overseas customers, Diana returned to college to get a master's degree in international trade for small business.

"Don't just read magazine articles; go back to school," she advises. "You need to be with people who want to do what you do."

Diana originally tried to find a distributor in Denmark because she had lived in the country for a year. Danes were interested only in butter cookies, however, not the Fudgy Chocolate Chunk cookies, Luscious Lemon Coconut cookies, Zesty Mandarin Orange Almond cookies, Macadamia Nut Chunk cookies, or other selections in Diana's Cookies' collection.

"Large companies can [export] on their own, but small companies can get so much help from the government," Diana says, referring to an important alliance with the U.S. Department of Commerce. Diana paid $1,700 plus travel expenses to participate in a trade mission to Northern Ireland in 1995. She and executives from 15 other American companies met business representatives from all over Ireland. For Diana, that led to a well-published partnership with a Northern Ireland cookie company in 1996. She agreed to introduce that baker's crackers into the United States, and it would make and distribute her cookies throughout Europe.

"I believe in long-standing relationships," Diana says. "Relationships are everything in business."

Relationships you can trust are especially important in international trade, she says. The distance alone, plus language and cultural barriers, make exporting different from tracking U.S. markets.

"You can't check on things overseas like you can domestically. Here, I jump in my car and drive to the bakery," she says. "You have to rely on the partner at the other end to jump if problems arise. It's time and money. You can't fly overseas all the time."

Diana learned this lesson the hard way when her Irish partner ran into financial problems a year into their agreement and eventually closed.

Now that she has spent the better part of the 1990s obtaining international trademarks for the Diana's California Cookies name and logo and developing relationships on three continents, Diana is not about to abandon the globalization of her products.

Through an alliance with a Hong Kong distributor, the cookies recently were introduced into mainland China. She also is working on strategic partnerships with other companies to sell to the United Kingdom, Europe, Mexico, and Japan.

"Originally, [exporting] takes longer than domestic deals," Diana says, "but once you start, the opportunities are endless."

# 84. FIND YOUR PIONEERS

Establish relationships with distributors and
other people who believe in your new product
enough to pioneer it nationwide.

■ ■ ■

The buyer for the large retail chain confessed that he used Ronn King's paint stirrer all the time at home, but he wouldn't stock it in his stores. King's company, Site-b, in Spokane, Washington, was just another one-product manufacturer in an age when large retailers and distributors want to limit their number of suppliers. They would rather buy a thousand products from one supplier than two each from 500 different manufacturers.

All inventors know the frustrations associated with turning their ideas into tangible products. The fact that retailers then greet their brainchildren with indifference or hostility chases many away.

Ronn spent 15-hour days for more than a year trying to break through this final barrier to market. But he couldn't do it alone. Credible salespeople had to be willing to be the first—the pioneers, as Ronn calls them—to take on a product with unproven customer appeal.

It all began when Ronn, looking for a better way to stir paint, attached a metal stick on a plastic cylinder that looked like a pet rodent's exercise wheel. Slats on the cylinder stir the paint quickly and completely when the stick is turned. Its appearance inspired the invention's name: the Squirrel Mixer.

Initially, Ronn tried to sell directly to buyers for major home-improvement retailers. One after another turned him down.

To prove that customers would buy the Squirrel Mixer, Ronn started selling it by mail order and persuaded some independent paint stores to carry it. Soon salespeople for distribution companies saw the Squirrel Mixer in several stores and started asking about it. Even then, however, their bosses didn't call Ronn; he had to call them.

One breakthrough came from a buyer who rejected the Squirrel Mixer, but referred Ronn to a manufacturer's representative that carries dozens of products for many companies. The representative not only liked the Squirrel Mixer enough to carry it in his line, he gave Ronn the names of sales representatives in other geographic areas. These pioneering independent representatives helped Ronn get the product into stores and attract distributors. That distribution relationship is important because while independent representatives take orders for a product, distributors actually buy it and stock it in their warehouses—a real cash-flow plus.

But distributors must make money too. Generally, they look for products that are similar to other products in their lines or that will sell in huge volume. Minus such an attraction, however, a distributor might accept a product that has a high profit margin and falls in a lucrative niche market the distributor wants to expand. The manufacturer also might have to offer incentives, such as one free case of product for every ten ordered or money for co-op advertising. Even after distributors and retailers add on their profit margins, though, the product still must sell for a price consumers will pay.

Ronn, with the help of his pioneers, sold 60,000 mixers in the first year and moved into the Home Depot chain. He also signed agreements with major paint companies, such as Red Devil, to put their labels on his product, which opened their distribution channels to the Squirrel Mixer and moved it into even more stores.

Still, even with a proven product, selling to major retailers is a continuing problem, Ronn says. Many retailers and distributors sit on the sidelines waiting for the small manufacturer to sell product rights to a big company or sign private-label agreements like Site-b's with Red Devil.

Ronn has had the good fortune to have people ask for different types and sizes of the Squirrel Mixer for uses he never imagined. Some factories want to attach a steel mixer to large motors to stir thousand-gallon drums of coatings and other materials. Food makers want Squirrel Mixers for commercial baking.

But those industries have completely different sales representatives and distributors, so Ronn is starting to build new relationships all over again.

# 85. BUILD WITH BOARDS

### A board of outside advisers can help an entrepreneur grow the business faster and smarter.

■ ■ ■

Leroy Knuths was a partner at one of the nation's largest accounting firms, but what he really wanted to do was run his own company—a manufacturing company, not another accounting practice. In 1980, he and some partners bought Rosco Manufacturing, which makes road maintenance equipment, and moved it to Madison, South Dakota.

"I wanted to form an outside board of advisers from the beginning, but my partners weren't interested," Leroy says. "I finally had to buy them out in order to set up an outside board."

Major corporations have boards of directors, but few entrepreneurs realize the value of an informal board of advisers even in a small company. This group doesn't dictate, it counsels and collaborates. If put together properly, the advisers bring experience, knowledge, and objectivity that the business owner lacks.

"I was very selective with whom I asked to be on my board," Leroy says.

Rosco Manufacturing's board of advisers has three members. One is the former president of a Rosco competitor. Leroy knew his adviser's abilities well, and the advisor knew Rosco well. The second adviser is a business owner with strong sales and marketing skills. Originally, the third adviser was a technical expert in manufacturing for the road construction industry. When he retired in 1997, the adviser recommended another technical expert.

Some business owners have more advisers, depending on their needs; however, large groups can be unwieldy. Besides, "It's not easy to recruit people of this caliber," Leroy says. "Part of the attraction for them is your own credibility and reputation."

Rosco's advisers meet quarterly, and Leroy pays them $1,000 apiece. Other entrepreneurs whose companies are young or financially strapped pay less or just buy lunch for their advisers. These experts usually aren't in it for the money. Some companies issue stock to their advisers. Leroy didn't take that route because he didn't want his advisers to have a financial interest in the advice they gave. Also, stock ownership raises liability issues that many advisers want to avoid.

"They have a lot of insight because they are objective," Leroy says. "They don't get hung up on details."

To make best use of a board of advisers, a business owner must be strong enough that the board doesn't domineer or pursue personal agendas. However, the owners also must want and use the help offered. Many business owners are secretive about their company operations; however, if they want their advisory boards to be useful, they must be candid, willing to share information, and open to change.

"You must be genuinely interested," Leroy says. "They only come on board on the condition that you listen to them."

With his board's help, Leroy has almost doubled the company, and has expanded sales overseas, including Russia, which suffers economically, in part, because its road infrastructure is so poor that products cannot be moved easily from plant to market. Rosco Manufacturing makes asphalt distributors, sweepers, rollers, and other large equipment to build and repair the country's roads.

"My board of advisers injected a whole lot of great ideas on the marketing side and the manufacturing side," Leroy says. "I knew we needed more sales emphasis, and they certainly supported that. They helped me hire a new sales manager."

The most difficult part about working with outside advisers is setting aside personal ego and sensitivities.

"You have to have broad shoulders and thick skin," Leroy says, "and be willing to bite your tongue at times."

**70.** You pay your employees good money; give them guidance, then give them a chance to shine.

**71.** Never reinvent the wheel. Figure out who has been through the situation you currently face, and ask for help.

**72.** Develop your own training programs, tailored to your specific skill needs.

**73.** Good salaries, customized perks, and a nurturing work environment are cheaper than constantly hiring and training new employees.

**74.** Ask job applicants work-related questions, and provide problem-solving scenarios. Carefully listen to and analyze their responses.

**75.** It's hard to admit your weaknesses, but your candor may be one of the most important tools in hiring the right employees to strengthen your company.

**76.** Pay is a reward and should also be used as an incentive to achieve even greater work.

**77.** If you want employees to follow the rules, you'd better make darned sure they know what those rules are and the consequences for breaking them.

**78.** Two heads may be better than one, but yours is the one that will be chopped off if you make legal mistakes; therefore, continually study the laws and regulations affecting your business.

**79.** Complementary skills and matching belief systems make for good partnerships as well as marriages.

**80.** Never enter a partnership without a written partnership agreement, with each side consulting its own attorney.

**81.** Fill your management team with the most skilled specialists you can find, not cronies and cousins.

**82.** Home-based entrepreneurs aren't superhuman. You need help balancing personal and professional life, just like everyone else.

**83.** Find other companies that need you as much as you need them. It's a match made in heaven.

**84.** Look for assistance from other entrepreneurs who succeed by finding fledgling companies and products with great potential.

**85.** Seek the advice of experienced managers and entrepreneurs—then listen to them.

# PART 6

# MARKETING

■ ■ ■

**M**oney is the most obvious new-business need, and marketing is the most overlooked. In fact, marketing may be more essential than money. No one will give you money until they know you exist, and no one will know your company exists until you announce it. That's marketing. Just as significant, without marketing no one will know that your products and services satisfy his greatest desires and overcome his greatest fears.

Marketing begins with market research—knowing who wants what you're selling. It continues with targeting—figuring out who's most likely to buy. And it moves on to planning—determining how your likely customer makes buying decisions.

The well-crafted marketing plan combines the benefits of your products and services with the right combination of message delivery channels. Today's consumer is so bombarded with information that you need to choose carefully what you say and how, when, and where you say it.

I can feel you tensing up already. Relax. Many business owners discover that marketing becomes the greatest fun of their work lives.

# 86. THE MYTH OF THE BETTER MOUSE TRAP

Just because you build a better
mousetrap doesn't mean the world
will beat a path to your door.

■ ■ ■

Engineer David Giuliani was skeptical when University of Washington professors David Engel and Roy Martin asked him to head a company to develop their new electric toothbrush. The home electric toothbrush market was large—$184 million in annual sales—but so was the competition. Braun, Teledyne, and Bausch & Lomb all had viable entries backed by far more money than this trio had.

Yeah, but Engel's and Martin's idea was to blast bacteria with sound waves, not scrub it off. Unfortunately, their technology didn't work.

David Giuliani continued his day job at Abbott Labs and spent his free time turning that idea into a viable product for his new company, Optiva Corp. in Bellvue, Washington. He spent two years developing a workable technology for the Sonicare Toothbrush—and that was the easy part.

Most consumers don't go looking for new products, especially $130 toothbrushes. They must be wooed to a new product or way of doing things with strong, continuous, well-conceived marketing.

"It's hard to get a new product to market," David says. "We had more roadblocks than many, but, on average, it's what one should expect in developing a new product."

Optiva lacked the huge marketing budgets of its larger competitors, so it decided to market to dentists by advertising in dental journals and hiring a few salespeople to call on the dentists. The company didn't have a great deal of quantitative data, but cofounder David Engel was a periodontist with a good industry reputation. And dentists who tried Sonicare swore by it.

"Marketing has to be done in sequence and at a certain rate," David Giuliani says. "If we moved too fast, we would have irritated dentists."

While dentists would push the market, Optiva wanted to create some consumer interest to pull it.

"Even today," David says, "many dentists take Sonicare seriously because they have had a patient whose gums look great, and when they ask, 'What are you doing, flossing?' the patients says, 'I bought a Sonicare.'"

Optiva began creating this consumer interest by mailing ads in millions of credit card billing statements. The result was only 11 sales. Obviously, Sonicare's benefits couldn't be pitched in a brief ad; therefore, in 1995, the company turned to infomercials—30-minute program-like commercials that heavily stress research results, which the company had by this time, and expert recommendations.

"We had a few testimonials, but the average viewer would just think we paid someone to say good things, so the experts and research were more important," David says.

A year earlier, Optiva sponsored Paul Harvey's radio show. Harvey often does his own commercials, and his audience is of an age when dental disease is a common problem, David says. "We didn't have a reputation, so we needed a spokesperson with a preexisting reputation, like Paul Harvey has."

By 1996, Sonicare held 33 percent of the U.S. electric toothbrush market, second only to Braun. In 1997, David was named the national Small Business Person of the Year by the U.S. Small Business Administration, partly for having grown the company to $100 million in sales with 250 employees and helping create another thousand jobs at surrounding small and mid-sized companies.

That is hardly the end of Optiva's story. The company is developing other products with sonics, including a new technology that David says will do an even better job of preventing gum disease. Of course, that will mean taking another "better mousetrap" to market.

# *87.* MARKETING NEEDS A PLAN, TOO

Even if your venture has a business plan,
it needs a strong marketing plan, too.

■ ■ ■

**K**athy Donoghue traveled a great deal as operations manager for a major computer company. During one trip, she read in an in-flight magazine about the National Association of Professional Organizers and thought she should start that type of consulting practice.

In 1988, she and partner Judy Nevins opened Another Alternative in Alden, New York. They have since established a second office in Sun City Center, Florida, to train, consult, and teach seminars on time management and the organizing process.

Although the partners wrote a business plan, which includes a section on marketing, the company would have attracted more business if they had written a much stronger, separate marketing plan, Kathy says.

"We all think we have the best thing to offer and everyone will realize it," she says. "But especially with a new service business, we have to sell ourselves and our services almost from scratch."

The marketing portion of most business plans plays a minor supporting role to issues of management, financing, and product or service. However, some experts argue that you can't really write a business plan until you have identified someone to buy what you want to sell. In fact, you should write a separate marketing plan each time you introduce a new product or service or enter a new market. The plan doesn't have to be very long or formal, but it should establish your strategy so you effectively reach the people most likely to buy from you.

Marketing has five elements: product (what you're selling), package, promotion (how you reach potential buyers), price, and place (where you'll sell the product and how you'll get it there). Different companies place different emphasis on these elements in their marketing.

The well-prepared marketing plan specifies what is unique about your product or service. It identifies the size of your expected market, by segment, and the share you can reasonably expect to capture. It lists major competitors, why customers buy from them, their sales, growth rates, and market shares. The plan describes your most likely customers, why they will buy from you, and which forms of promotion and advertising will most effectively reach them. And no marketing plan is complete without a timetable, budget, and means for measuring results.

Without a strong marketing plan, Another Alternative lacked an efficient, effective strategy for growing with limited funds.

"When we first started, people didn't know what we did. We had to work hard to establish the need in people's minds," Kathy says.

A strong marketing plan would have classified the most productive ways to educate potential clients to their need for organizational help.

"When I go in [to a client's buisiness] I wear different hats going through the [consulting] process. I start as analyst, then teacher and coach, then reviewer to make sure they keep on track," she says.

Kathy originally focused her attention on individuals rather than companies. "If people don't change, nothing changes," she explains. However, trying to train one person at a time isn't very lucrative and achieves limited results. To grow Another Alternative and accomplish bigger results for her clients, Kathy needed to help an entire department or company organize its strategies.

A marketing plan could have helped her identify that market sooner. As it was, Kathy started with small companies, then worked up to bigger projects and clients.

"The more work I did, the more people referred me," she says. "I taught a lot of seminars and workshops, which brought more business, but I couldn't become a presenter until I had the experience."

Kathy's strategy to obtain referrals could have been part of her marketing plan, too.

# 88. MARKETING IS AN INVESTMENT

Don't choose your marketing efforts
based on how much they cost.
Calculate the return on investment.

■ ■ ■

**W**hile working as an interviewer and job counselor in the early 1970s, Patty DeDominic loved listening to people's dreams and matching them to the right job. In a later job as a corporate trainer, she loved the interaction with business people. Later still she advised employment services. That's when Patty realized that instead of doing this work for other companies, she should do it for her own. In 1979 she opened PDQ Personnel Services as a temporary-employment agency in Los Angeles, California.

"I began consulting with staffing services, then I thought I should do it for myself," Patty says. "I would have gained more business sooner if I had invested money in marketing and business development from the start," Patty says.

Few new business owners who don't have marketing backgrounds think of business marketing as an investment. They look at a marketing plan's price tag, emit a low whistle, and say, "Wow! That's expensive." The truth is, they don't know whether it's expensive; they know what they expect to spend. In most cases, they don't have as much start-up capital as they need, but they don't know how much that marketing expenditure is worth to the company in terms of revenue, prestige, contacts, and visibility.

If you put $100 in a government-insured savings account at 3 percent interest, you know you'll have $103 at the end of the term. If you invest it in a gas exploration firm, you might triple your money or lose it all. You are weighing risk versus potential gain.

You can do the same when you look at marketing as an investment. You won't merely throw money into telephone directory ads, billboards, and direct mail pieces; you will assess the likelihood of getting business from those efforts. How much business? What kind of business? Will you get more business from a quarter-page ad in a newspaper or a trade journal? Once you have run the ad or sent the direct mail piece, you can evaluate the results in terms of value to your company to determine how you'll spend your marketing dollars next time. Marketing becomes an ever increasingly precise investment instead of money tossed into a black hole.

Patty and her staff now hold annual marketing strategy meetings. They weigh whether and how much money and effort PDQ Services should put into public relations, advertisements, and sales. Then they put their decisions in writing.

"We want to make sure that our strategy for the year is the backbone of all our marketing to reinforce and leverage our message," Patty says.

For example, if the strategy is to stress PDQ's quality services that have expanded into permanent placements and employee leasing, Patty chooses different media to get that message across.

"One year, we made a major commitment to radio advertising. The next, to billboards, direct mail, and telemarketing," she says.

Patty carefully monitors the business growth that can be attributed to each of her advertising efforts. This evaluation requires every marketing application to include some measurement means. That's why radio ads sometimes end with "mention this ad and get a 10 percent discount." That's why direct mail pieces often contain discount coupons. That's why some magazine ads list mailbox numbers for orders. The same ad in different publications has different mailbox numbers.

Sales may not be the only way you measure the worth of your marketing endeavors. Patty is on the boards for local, state, and women's business organizations, and PDQ Services gains visibility through those relationships. However, that time investment has value beyond the business bottom line.

"When there is an alignment between my personal beliefs and the organization's business purposes, I am much more likely to be involved and encourage my staff to be involved," Patty says.

# *89.* THE WORLD IS NOT YOUR MARKET

There's not enough money or time in the world for companies to market themselves successfully as all things to all people.

■ ■ ■

**A**s a college student in the 1970s, Martha Daniel wanted to run the information services department of a major corporation someday. However, after working her way up several corporate ladders, she thought she could do better as boss of the whole business. So in 1992, Martha launched Information Management Resources, Inc., to provide computer-consulting services to large corporations, including some of her old employers.

"When you're a new company, you're building your business off relationships. Whatever they want, you do," Martha says. "But I was absolutely too scattered."

Martha was like many new business owners: unwilling to focus on a niche for fear of missing a sale. So they waste time and money trying to sell everything to everyone. The result is often bankruptcy, burnout, or both.

"I needed a niche, so I looked back at the work we had done and saw the types of jobs we had done most," Martha says.

She defined several related services for the core business of Information Management Resources, based in Costa Mesa, California with offices in four other states and Washington, D.C. The company would concentrate on systems integration, training, financial and custom software, and solutions to the Year 2000 problem for computer systems. (Some hardware and software will read 2000 as 1900, potentially affecting everything from missile launchers to ATM machines.)

One of the company's original services that Martha let go was telecommunications because it didn't fit with company strengths or clients' demands. Martha wisely chose to hang on to related services, however, which enables Information Management Resources to gain additional work with existing clients. Past buyers are the most likely future buyers, so marketing to them costs a fraction of the expense of corralling new customers.

If Information Management Resources develops a piece of custom software, Martha explains, the client needs to have it integrated into the company's existing hardware and software system and to have employees trained to use it. Information Management Resources has the inside track of winning that additional work.

Such targeting shortens a company's sales cycle and devotes time and personal attention to the people most likely to buy a product or service.

"Narrowing my service offerings [in the beginning] would have enabled me to present a manageable marketing plan," Martha says. "Additionally, my clients would have viewed the business differently—as a specialist, not a generalist."

Specialists can command higher pay rates and attention than generalists. They also tend to have less competition.

You can develop a better understanding of your target market by asking yourself five Ws: *Who* is your customer? *What* does this customer need and want? *Where* will the customer expect to find you? *Why* will the customer choose you? *When* is the customer likely to have this need?

Timing, too, can influence a company's marketing focus. Martha emphasizes her company's ability to resolve the Year 2000 problem because her customers need it now. In fact, that division represents 35 percent of company work. She expects the need to continue for several years into the new century.

However, Martha acknowledges, at some point, the company probably will drop Year 2000 services from its marketing focus. Just as companies must focus on a niche to maximize their marketing dollars, they need to periodically evaluate the niche and adjust their services because customer needs and markets change continually.

# *90.*  THE VALUE
## OF DIVERSITY

Don't put all your eggs in one basket.
Marketing to a single customer makes a
company more vulnerable to economic swings.

■  ■  ■

**A**lthough Rafael Correa grew up working for the family-owned machine shop, he wanted to establish his own precision manufacturing company. So, in 1988, Rafael started Machining Technologies, Inc.— MaTech for short—in Salisbury, Maryland.

Rafael originally was a contract manufacturer for the military "because it was the biggest customer in the industry, and I was most familiar with it," he says. However, when he read the news headlines and learned of proposed federal budgets, Rafael knew that the Cold War was winding down and Congress was cutting military spending. If MaTech didn't find customers outside the military, it wouldn't survive.

"In the early 1990s, military purchases came to a halt," Rafael says. "We had contracts that ended midstream. It was a long, dry period."

A small supplier relying totally on one industry, even one as large as defense used to be in this country, finds itself in a precarious position. Recent history has proven that even giant corporations dependent on the defense sector have cut their operations dramatically and merged to survive. Thousands of small defense firms went out of business or converted to other activities. Rafael was determined to take the latter road.

A small firm must strike a delicate balance between finding a niche and diversifying enough to survive the inevitable ebbs and flows a single industry can experience. This balance is both a management and a marketing issue.

MaTech doesn't merely make parts to meet customers' specifications. Its niche is making customized precision parts and completely assembling the entire equipment. The military isn't unique in its willingness to contract for that combination of product and services. Rafael needed to identify and redirect his marketing efforts toward other industries that could see the value of his specialty and were willing to contract for it from an outside company.

"I looked at where the future growth in government spending would be. There were Environmental Protection Agency clean-up projects, transportation, and communication," Rafael says. "We needed to see which we could best serve with the infrastructure we had in place."

MaTech focused new marketing efforts toward the telecommunications, medical, and transportation industries. The company still does work for the military, but has decreased its dependency on the sector to about 50 percent of its business. That downward trend will continue, Rafael says.

Rafael took other steps to diversify MaTech's market beyond identifying other customers for the company's existing capabilities. A contract manufacturer makes parts designed and owned by its customers, but does not have products of its own, he points out. The manufacturer depends on other companies for anything it makes. And competition is fierce for these machining contracts.

"We are developing our own product for the automotive industry," Rafael says. "Rather than making for others what is already in the market, we will have product that is new to sell."

He is hopeful that this additional diversification of his company's skills will further reduce MaTech's susceptibility to one industry's economic fortunes—and misfortunes.

"All markets are cyclical," Rafael says. "With more diversity of clientele, you increase your possibilities of survival if one or more customers are in downturns."

# 91. THE RIGHT BALANCE OF TIME WELL SPENT

If you started your company because you love
the technical side of the business, practice
your marketing and presentation skills.

■ ■ ■

James Woo was a university researcher when he realized how wide the gap was between the basic research that went on in university labs and the ability to find some practical use for that research in the real world. So, in 1981, Jim formed InterScience, Inc., in Troy, New York, to bridge the gap.

InterScience employees do high-tech research and development under contract with the government and private companies. They have developed such projects as fiber optic medical instruments and night vision goggles.

"Most of the competition for our work comes from university Ph.D.s and engineers," Jim says. "We just decided to do it commercially instead of at a university, where the primary objective is teaching students, not commercializing ideas."

It is both InterScience's boon and bane that its researchers behave like, well, researchers.

"We would get turned on by exciting ideas, and we'd go off doing our thing, forgetting that if we were going to make money, somebody better want to buy it," Jim says.

Scientists and engineers aren't the only people who bury themselves in the technical side of their ventures and never get out and sell themselves, their ideas, or their services. Many inventors never get their ideas to market because they leave to others the nitty gritty work of turning the ideas into reality. Anyone who starts a business because he's good at some skill—from a plumber to a crafts manufacturer—is vulnerable to this temptation.

"It's a misconception that if you have outstanding ideas you will get contracts, especially if you're small," Jim says.

"Ours is a two-way street," he adds. "The people with projects have to know us before they will bring the projects to us, and if we have a good idea, we have to know where to sell it to get R&D funding."

Both require relationship building, so Jim, as president, finally had to relinquish time in the lab to beat InterScience's drums. He now spends more than half his time marketing for the company.

Entrepreneurs like Jim spend much of their time talking informally with people at business parties or industry meetings and formally during sales presentations. Jim needs to listen to what research and development projects his potential clients want and to tell InterScience's story well enough to win the contracts to do those projects. It's best for Jim and other entrepreneurs to speak for themselves because no one has the fire and enthusiasm that they do.

However, technically skilled business owners often must overcome one obstacle: shyness. The difference between them and glib marketeers is practice, whether alone or with a speech or drama coach. The goal is to hone a concise, compelling story about a company and its work that emphasizes the benefits to the buyer, not all the Bunsen burners and computers in the lab.

These gab sessions can be scary. The reassuring fact is that both your tale and your storytelling skills improve with practice. Don't be embarrassed to rehearse your story, run through trial question and answer sessions, videotape yourself, analyze your efforts with your speech coach, then videotape again. Over time, your delivery becomes animated. Awkward gestures become comfortable. You develop open body language, including making eye contact as you speak and not crossing your arms across your chest. However, if you're the quiet type, don't try to transform yourself into the class clown.

"I have been learning slowly to put greater emphasis on market demands for the technology we are developing," Jim says. "The market must drive our research instead of the other way around."

# *92.* CHECK YOUR FAVORITE

### Survey your market before you decide
### what products or services to offer.

■ ■ ■

**D**ave Markham, a former respiratory therapist, became so good at leading outdoor recreation trips that, in 1982, he and his wife, Sue Barney, decided to start their own travel adventure company—Venture Outdoors, in Hailey, Idaho. Dave kept his winter job at Boise State University until 1988, but each summer, he and Sue took tourists on kayaking, hiking, and bike tours.

"I had a good idea what I wanted to do, but that's where I goofed," Dave says. "I picked out activities that I was most qualified to do and most enjoyed doing. I finally realized that if I was going to survive, I had to be more realistic and find out what the public wanted to do. Then I could narrow it down to what I wanted to do that people were willing to pay for."

Many new business owners plunge into their enterprises without really asking whether anyone is willing to pay for the proposed products or services. Surveys of the marketplace can save those business owners willing to heed the results a lot of money and frustration.

"I couldn't afford an expensive survey, but I did read travel industry magazines to find out what the trends were," Dave says. "Unfortunately, I read what I wanted to read and ignored a lot of useful information at first."

For example, Dave learned that kayaking was growing in popularity, and because he had been kayaking since 1968, offering a kayak trip seemed like a good fit. However, Dave got few registrations for his trips of intermediate skill to Alaska. Listening to prospective customers convinced him to change the activity to a trip for beginners, which has been quite successful. In fact, Dave reevaluated all the vacations he offered for rugged adventurers.

"Now, we're a cushy wilderness experience," Dave says. Tour guests are treated to trail meals of raspberry French toast, orange beef, and chocolate cream pie, for example.

Although Dave didn't have a big budget for formal market surveys, he started asking anyone who called Venture Outdoors' toll-free telephone number what he or she wanted in an adventure vacation. He sent out surveys to everyone on the company's mailing list, compiled from inquiries and past tour guests. Every brochure includes a short survey that the recipient can fill out and send back.

"You can't ask too many questions, [though,] or people won't respond," Dave says. But every little bit of information helps, and when diligently logged and categorized, it adds up to sizeable market research.

"When we finally get people on a trip, we give them more than we promised and then hope they will provide us with feedback at the end of the trip, good and bad," Dave says.

Adventure travel is the fastest growing segment of the vacation industry, and many people want to take these trips with family. However, different members of each family have different levels of skill and desire for challenge, Dave says.

"Maybe Dad and son want more aggressive biking side trips than Mom and daughter want," he says. "We have modified every trip to accommodate those types of requests."

You never know enough to stop surveying current and potential customers, Dave says. Although Idaho weather pretty much confines Venture Outdoors to summer trips in the state, Dave and Sue have added winter trips to Baja, Mexico, because people requested them.

"And to grow the company, we can't continue just as a summer program," Dave says. "We have to go outside Idaho."

# *93.* THE INFORMAL PIPELINE

Small-business owners must understand how
their potential customers form business
relationships and award contracts.

■ ■ ■

**A**ll his adult life, Ernest Camacho had been self-employed, doing everything from owning a chain of liquor stores to selling insurance. As an appointee of the Carter Administration, Ernest traveled the country studying the economic issues affecting small minority-owned firms. That experience was the foundation of his next entrepreneurial venture, Pacifica Services, Inc., which he opened in Pasadena, California, in 1979.

Originally, his company served as a consultant helping small companies understand the federal government's program for economically disadvantaged firms. Soon Ernest decided Pacifica should compete for government contracts itself. Although he didn't have an engineering degree, Ernest hired engineers and other specialists to fashion Pacifica into an engineering, construction, and program management firm. His eye was on lucrative contracts with the federal departments of defense and transportation.

It became apparent that contract awards depended a great deal on relationships. Even finding out about potential work depended on whom you knew.

"There was a real old boys' network in place. By the time a project was published in *Commerce Business Daily,* the work had already been awarded," Ernest says.

Most small-business owners who set their sights on contracts with the federal government and major corporations have discovered they must spend years marketing and building relationships before they start to make inroads into these lucrative areas. Pacifica itself lumbered along with about 14 employees for four years. Ernest kept the company alive by accepting consulting work and small jobs.

"No one hands contracts to you," he says. "You have to be competitive. You use everything you can to develop those relationships."

Small firms on this big-game hunt often work through national trade associations. They attend government procurement conferences and specialty trade shows, peruse *Commerce Business Daily* where the needs of government agencies are printed, and put their names on bid lists to be notified when government agencies have work. They make friends with the small-business specialists that many government agencies and major corporations employ. These liaisons don't make buying decisions, however, so the small-business owner must find the purchasing agents within these agencies and companies—not an easy task. That's why learning this process takes years, although Ernest believes if he were to do it again, it wouldn't take him so long to maneuver through the contract labyrinth.

After four years of cultivating federal buyers, Pacifica hit pay dirt—a $3 million contract at Travis Air Force Base. Practically overnight, the company grew to 150 employees. Once Ernest made the breakthrough, many other large government contracts followed.

His formula for success in winning big contracts isn't secret; it's persistence, targeted marketing, and relationship building. And once a contract is awarded, his formula for success changes: deliver top quality; otherwise, no other contracts will follow.

"I used to spend a lot of my time back east marketing our services to procurement officers in the federal government," he says. "It was a lot of work, but it certainly paid off. We still maintain a presence in Washington, D.C."

In fact, as federal spending dwindled, Ernest applied his persistence in relationship building to a new market—major corporations and other levels of government. Now half the work of the 450-employee company is with private corporations, and half is with government agencies.

"It's a game of marketing yourself and your company," Ernest says.

But you have to understand your market to know the rules of the game.

# *94.* HOMEMADE MARKETING

Lack of money is no excuse not to market
your business. Legwork and time
must substitute for money.

■  ■  ■

**P**earl White was an executive secretary for a large homebuilder when the company was sold.

"The company and industry were changing. I had dreamed of owning a business for a long time; this seemed like the right time to make that dream come true," she says.

On January 1, 1979, Pearl opened the doors of Confidante Keys, an Irvine, California, secretarial and administrative services firm. Later she opened another company, 1st Impression Resume Service.

Pearl started with $1,000 in vacation pay from her previous employer. She was on such a tight budget that she didn't have money for advertising. Without it, though, she knew Confidante Keys was headed for an early burial. Therefore, Pearl's time and effort had to make up for the money she lacked.

Pearl's office was located in an industrial park, so she began by typing up her own simple flyer describing her services, qualifications, and location, then hand delivered them to every business in the park. That brought a handful of clients. Next, she joined the local chamber of commerce. That brought a few more projects. She also agreed to be the paid coordinator for a leads group, which was a stable source of income for many years and showcased her abilities for member businesses.

"Every little bit helps," Pearl says.

All marketing benefits a new business to some degree, but nothing in marketing works all the time. Many different, even small, efforts executed in a coordinated and consistent way build business. In fact, small-business owners often find that when they stop marketing, their business slows down within two months.

As Pearl discovered, a financially strapped entrepreneur can still find many inexpensive ways to promote business. For example, Pearl advises asking your existing reservoir of friends for the names of potential customers, then following up on those names. The average customer needs seven contacts before he buys, so continually contact the same people in fresh ways rather than calling or mailing to a person just once before moving on. Even today, Pearl hands out business cards and calendars with her company name imprinted on them, although she no longer needs to hand deliver flyers around the neighborhood. You also can distribute discount coupons, informative articles or useful checklists. Your contacts with customers are limited by your creativity, not your pocketbook.

Once you have a few customers, find out more about them so you can offer additional services or products that meet their needs and interests, Pearl says. Call potential customers to let them know about your sales or when you add a new service or product line for which they have expressed interest.

Pearl now gets most of her business through referrals from existing and former clients. You can encourage people to give you more referrals by asking who they know who might want or need your products or services. Ask satisfied clients for referrals, too. Don't sit back and expect busy people to refer to you without prompting.

Pearl has found that her type of business needs to be listed in the telephone directory, but those advertisements can be expensive. However, even a lower cost bold-lettered listing has worked better than nothing, she says. Over the years, Pearl also has discovered that she gets better results and saves money by listing in fewer directories within her geographic area than spreading her dollars over every telephone directory in the entire region.

Personalized marketing has kept Pearl in business for two decades.

"It has been an education, expanded my understanding of my capabilities," she says. "I've been able to help a lot more people than if I were in one company."

# *95.* CUSTOMERS BY MAIL

Direct mail advertising can save a
lot of marketing money by targeting
the right customers.

■ ■ ■

**T**alk about a mismatch: Dick Seaholm majored in art in college, but worked for 40 years in the air-conditioning industry. He hated his job; however, he had a family to raise and felt he couldn't take any chances. Finally, though, Dick made a career change, trying his hand at sales until new ownership bankrupted the company. He then taught goal-setting seminars until attendance dried up during the recession of the early 1990s.

For a while, Dick helped out his son-in-law, who was a police officer doing screen printing on the side. Then Dick learned that the local quick-print shop was getting rid of its department that applied heat transfers to T-shirts, mugs, and signs. So, in 1995, Dick sold some real estate holdings and borrowed from a family trust to open Rich Mar Transfers, a custom heat-transfer print service, in his home in Costa Mesa, California. He and his wife, Lynn, built a modest business through networking, ads in telephone directories, and word of mouth.

But direct mail advertising could have identified and reached Rich Mar's best prospects more quickly and completely for faster growth, Dick says.

"The biggest obstacle we had to overcome was recognition," he says. "Our motto is 'our minimum order is one,' but people who needed small orders didn't know we existed."

Direct mail, done improperly, is junk mail. Done correctly, it is like using an advertising rifle instead of a shotgun.

Before embarking on his first direct mail campaign in 1998, Dick spent a great deal of time identifying what and to whom he wanted to sell. He decided to emphasize his ability to make vinyl banners and signs. His targets were construction companies, property managers, insurance companies, and restaurants, which he identified by their Standard Industrial

Classification (SIC) codes, company sizes, and geographic locations. If you're targeting companies, mail order pros recommend addressing the piece to a position instead of a name because people change jobs too often for commercial mailing lists to keep up.

A U.S. Postal Service study found that people open their mail according to the return address. Direct mail must have a return address, but it doesn't have to be in the envelope's upper left-hand corner. So many direct mail professionals print the required information on the inside. The pros often send direct mail individually addressed with first-class stamps instead of printed bulk mail. Personalized addresses and first-class postage are more expensive, but the envelope is opened more often.

Rich Mar Transfers uses direct mail to help level out the business's ups and downs. The company is swamped in the first quarter of the year, putting players' names on uniforms for youth sports leagues. But, without marketing, business slows in April. That's when Dick sends out his direct mail.

A single mailing is a waste of money. Dick mails at least four times to the same list, which greatly increases response. He also mails just 2,000 pieces at a time to avoid attracting more work than he can handle. A company that stresses how it turns orders around quickly can hardly afford to make first-time customers wait even a few weeks.

"I've seen other companies that got to doing too much and were overwhelmed," Dick says. "Once you have a customer base, that's your first loyalty."

# *96.* THE RIGHT NETWORK

While networking is a valuable marketing
tool, not all groups are equally effective
in bringing you business.

■ ■ ■

**A**drienne Escoe worked in management for a large, international aerospace company, gaining experience in systems and procedures, administration, and human resources. But when defense cutbacks brought continual downsizing to the company, Adrienne decided, in 1995, to open her own consulting practice, Escoe/Bliss Communications, in Seal Beach, California.

Adrienne's goal was to help companies create the documentation, records, policies, and procedures they need to meet legal requirements, quality standards, and corporate goals.

Companies require a surprising array of documents for everything from ISO 9000 certification for international sales to employee handbooks to technical manuals, Adrienne explains.

Adrienne believed that networking would be one of the best marketing tools to build her practice. "However, I should have been more selective about the networking groups I joined," she says. "I spent a lot of time with groups that were more oriented to retail or very small businesses, and my business works with corporate clients."

Basically, networking is building relationships. People do business with people they know. Unfortunately, business networking sometimes gets a negative image from those who apply hard sales tactics to every conversation.

The best networkers spend more time listening than talking. They learn what others need, then figure out how they can help meet that need. Sometimes that help is just a referral to some other company. Sometimes it leads to a contract.

Too many new business owners like Adrienne leap into many groups that have no real prospects for building their businesses. No single group is ideal for every person, and each organization has a different personality and a constituency that matches certain business needs. Some people love the social interaction of certain groups so much that they're reluctant to give them up, even if they offer little business potential. That's fine; everyone needs fun. However, you shouldn't kid yourself that you are using that time to build your business. Other groups may be sources of useful information, but not good sources of business contacts or referrals.

A small-business owner has a limited amount of time, so every marketing effort should be efficient and effective. That's what Adrienne had to accept about some of the business groups she joined originally.

"It was a time management issue," she says. "Even a breakfast meeting, considering travel time and getting ready, takes half the day."

Adrienne found that her most likely clients are professionals who are decision makers for corporations, not retailers or small service businesses.

Finding organizations that are popular with those types of businesspeople has been a long study in trial and error, she says.

"I still occasionally attend some groups' events for information, but not as a source of clients," she says.

The personalities of certain organizations change as the leadership changes. Once-effective groups wane; others grow. Business owners should continually reassess whether the time and money they spend with a group is worthwhile.

Involvement also is an important part of relationship building. You just can't show up at meetings once a month and expect others in the crowd to know and trust you. That trust grows as you work together.

"With me, many exposures in a few groups is more effective that once in many different groups," Adrienne says. "I attend meetings, but I also do a lot of speaking at conferences, place ads in professional journals, and write articles. I think that helps build my relationships and credibility."

# *97.* YOU HAVE TEN SECONDS

### You must develop a pithy, appealing description of your business.

■ ■ ■

Libby Jason entertained a great deal, but didn't have much time to plan and prepare for parties because she traveled so much in her work.

"I thought there had to be someone who could come in and make the party special and high quality," she says.

Libby finally decided that that someone might as well be her. With a fine arts background and a marketing degree, she knew she didn't want to spend the rest of her life selling contact lenses for an ophthalmology company. So in 1982, Libby started Your Home Plate in Coto de Caza, California, to design and set up customized table settings for parties.

Libby soon discovered that her business was so unusual that no one understood it.

"I joined a networking group to practice getting up and describing my business, but after even 30 or 40 times, people still couldn't figure out what

I did," Libby says. "They kept telling me, 'I couldn't understand what you do until I went to one of your parties.'"

That lack of understanding hurt Libby's business growth. In this hurry-up society, most people give you ten seconds before their attention wanders to "What's for dinner?" or "Do I know that guy in the green tie?" Yet one of the most common questions people ask is what you do for a living. The ability to tell them in a quick, compelling way that perks their interest is the best marketing tool small-business owners have every time they step into an elevator, stand in a grocery line, or attend a business gathering.

You try to create a memorable image with logos, company names, and advertising; your self-introduction should do the same. For example, a tax preparer might say, "I help people keep more of what they make." An insurance sales executive can say, "I'm in the protection racket." A merger and acquisition adviser can declare, "In my business, one plus one equals one." And a loan officer might advise, "Think of me as your money."

"Creating the right self-introduction really took a long time and more work than you'd think," Libby says. She also has learned to vary her descriptions, depending on the situations and the listeners. "One time, I will say, 'I own a business that does creative tabletop designs and upscale rentals for parties.' Or 'I'm in the entertaining business, helping you entertain and enjoy your party.' Or 'I own an upscale party rental company.'

"If I'm talking to a man, I never use the word 'decorating' or 'designer,'" Libby adds. "They're just not interested, as if they think it's too fluffy." She knew they weren't interested because they never asked follow-up questions when she said she did tabletop design. Women always asked, "What's that?"

If your ten-second introduction does its job in creating interest in your listener, you must be ready to provide more information about your company that will stir up even more interest. For example, Libby might describe one of her parties—like the *Titanic* party, where she decorated with a water wall and an ice sculpture iceberg and designed each table for a different section of the ship or a different character in the movie.

Libby's self-introductions have become real marketing tools for Your Home Plate and a companion personalized chef service, What a Dish. Now she gets immediate comprehension—and attention—from her listeners.

# *98.* SIGN OF YOUR TIMES

Without a sign, a new business is
invisible even on a busy street.

■ ■ ■

**A**fter more than two decades of selling vegetable seeds in western New York state, Harold Ford was laid off. He investigated several options and had decided to buy a packing and shipping franchise when he saw a for-sale ad for a newly built independent shop. So in 1996, at the age of 59, Harold opened Postal Copy Center in a strip mall in Meridian, Idaho.

At the time, Harold didn't even think about the importance of having a sign visible from the busy thoroughfare on which the shopping center sat. Neither did his fellow small-business tenants or the landlord.

"Signage is so important," Harold says. "How can people find your business if you don't have a sign? I don't know how I overlooked it."

Despite other types of marketing, which included mailing coupons for free keys to new homeowners in the area, Postal Copy Center struggled to get established because of its invisibility on a busy street. Harold did put a sign on his shop, but traffic moves too fast to see it.

"We pay rent based on being on this busy street, but we don't get any benefit from it," he says.

When Harold and another merchant put out a temporary banner that violated the city's sign ordinance, Harold had to remove the banner and pay a $350 fine.

"Investigate your city's sign ordinance before you go into business," Harold recommends. "Most of them are cracking down on signs, eliminating pole signs altogether, limiting their size."

And although it's not a problem for Postal Copy Center, some landlords also have sign restrictions in their leases.

Because Harold's landlord was too busy to obtain the permits or order the sign, Harold and five other small tenants spent more than a year getting the city to approve and issue permits for a stucco monument sign, which sits on the ground. Postal Copy Center's portion on that sign is one foot by two feet for the cost of $400.

"But anything helps," Harold says.

Actually, a sign's limited size is a benefit. Sign experts say that few words are best because the average person looks at a sign for less than a second; the size of the letter is more important. Two-inch-high letters can be read at 50 feet, but if city ordinances allow it, letters should be three feet high to be read at a thousand feet.

Colors and letter style affect a sign's readability, too. Red and yellow are the most visible colors, and short, thick letters are easier to read than thin letters close together. Postal Copy Center's letters are red and black on Lucite, which is lighted from inside for greater visibility.

It's fortunate that Harold didn't insist that the sign convey everything Postal Copy Center does, from packaging to tax preparation to notary public sevices—and sells, including office supplies and cards. He just wanted a sign to alert drivers to the center's existence. Once customers have found him, Harold has been able to increase steadily the amount each spends in his center because of its wide variety of services and products.

Harold and the other merchants couldn't place their sign on the busy street because of a property ownership dispute, however, so they had to settle for a location on a side street with a fifth as much traffic. However, that street will be widened eventually, which will increase traffic and the number of people who see the sign, Harold says.

# *99.*    SPEAK UP

Public speaking and seminars help
establish credibility and visibility for
owners of service businesses.

■  ■  ■

Don McCrea spent 28 years working in the computer industry as a systems and product manager. However, he realized in 1990 that his employer was too dependent on aerospace and defense contracts at a time when both were shrinking. Determined to prepare himself to start a consulting firm when the inevitable layoff came, Don enrolled in a business doctorate program at his employer's expense.

When he was laid off in 1992, Don already had the home office set up for Decisioneering, an Irvine, California, marketing and strategic planning consulting firm.

"It's critical for anyone in business consulting to establish visibility and credibility frequently and quickly," Don says. "I should have found ways to do more speaking engagements sooner. They are critical to a consultant's success."

While some people make livings giving speeches and seminars, large numbers of owners of small service businesses like Don find that these public presentations are important marketing tools for building their full-time work. If these speeches are well done, they establish the owners as experts in their fields and reach targeted audiences of potential clients.

For Don, fear of public speaking was not the issue that it is for some people. He has taught college undergraduate, graduate, and executive business courses. Although that teaching experience enhanced his consulting credibility, public speeches and seminars would have grown his reputation and his practice much faster, Don says.

Business owners who want to use speeches as oral marketing tools must treat the projects with the same seriousness and professionalism that they bring to their companies. Research, preparation, and practice are essential if they want to attract speaking invitations.

Fledgling speakers usually must start by speaking to groups that are not ideal for business purposes, Don observes. The ideal group has members who can help the business owner and whom the owner can help. However, any speeches are good experience. The more you speak, the better you get, and the more likely you are to attract invitations from your target audiences.

How do you identify your ideal audience? First, identify your target market, then look for groups for that industry. Find out when and where they meet by reading calendar listings in newspapers, magazines, and industry publications. Ask potential clients what groups they join. Then contact these groups for the names of their program chairpersons, and send letters about your speech topics, qualifications, and availability for presentations.

Speakers and seminar leaders must define topics that showcase their expertise and also appeal to large numbers of people—preferably those who will want to buy a speaker's services.

Don, for example, is a marketing expert. His skill lies in helping a company target its marketing toward customers who already know they need, want, and can afford the company's products or services. Marketing with a how-to emphasis is a popular topic on the speaking circuit among business groups.

When you speak to business or civic groups, you must keep self-promotion to a minimum during your presentations. Many hosting groups demand it. However, you can and should write handouts, books, and other publications that enhance your presentation, boost your credibility, and—with a simple address and phone number tag line—promote your business.

Rather than develop a formal seminar, Don has gained visibility and credibility by becoming active in area chambers of commerce and small-business committees. As an officer of these groups, he often gives informal presentations before large crowds.

Public speaking is a more subtle marketing exposure with more subtle results. Still, Don says, the return is many times the investment.

# 100. 'NETTING CUSTOMERS

The Internet is an increasingly valuable
marketing tool for small businesses.

■ ■ ■

After retiring from the military in 1977, Michael Fritz took $2,000 of his own money to establish Dentrep 2000 in San Antonio, Texas, to repair ultrasonic cleaners and make related products used by dental labs and jewelers.

"Like all small businesses, I was completely underfunded," Mike says.

Without a big bankroll, Mike didn't have much of a marketing program. Survival was a daily struggle as Dentrep, which also goes by the name Lone Star Technical Service, grew mostly by word of mouth.

"I wish I could have advertised on the Internet a lot sooner," Mike says. "It has been our most productive advertising dollar by far."

The Internet was not an option when Mike started his business because this worldwide connection of computers was the province of university scientists and government agencies until the 1990s. Then the World Wide Web made access to the Internet easier, leading to a commercial explosion of the system. By 1997, the Internet boasted 320 million Web pages, with more companies and entrepreneurs adding new ones daily.

As soon as Lone Star Technical put up its site, it started attracting customers in Australia, Switzerland, England, and Germany—not bad for a two-man shop. In fact, one of the Internet's most appealing features for small companies is that they can appear to be as big and professional as IBM. Like Lone Star Technical, small companies can reach global markets without international sales forces or huge advertising budgets.

A Web site provides potential customers with 24-hour access to information about your company, its products, and its services at a lower price than a toll-free phone service or fax-back system. However, a Web site gives your company no more access to the 50 million Internet users than a mail-order company has access to the 250 million U.S. Postal Service users.

You must work at making a Web site a useful marketing tool for your company. Before setting it up, think through what you want the site to accomplish and how it fits into your overall marketing plan. A Web site is not a get-rich-quick scheme, and it shouldn't be your sole marketing effort.

Lone Star Technical started out renting inexpensive space on a service provider's computer, which gave the firm a site under the host's domain name. Lone Star Technical's resulting Uniform Resource Locator (URL), or address, in the format of http://domain name/file name, was long and difficult to remember. That made it hard for 'net surfers to find. Mike later switched to a site that gave Lone Star Technical its own domain name. However, even with the old, cumbersome URL, Mike was able to make his site more visible by establishing hyperlinks with many dental and jeweler sites. He also signed up with search engines that help Internet users find what they're looking for.

"I've gotten enough spam [unwanted e-mail ads] to fill a sandwich from companies claiming they can get your site to the top of search engines' lists," Mike says. "Don't waste your money. You can do it yourself for free."

Lone Star Technical's Web site explains its products and services. It also allows customers to e-mail the firm directly from the site or call the listed toll-free phone number. Other companies use their Web sites to boost customer service, communicate with employees, attract job applicants, and cross-promote products and services with strategic partners.

A high-tech company might need a flashy Web site with dancing icons, but many companies like Lone Star Technical find their customers don't care about such features and don't want to wait for these graphics to load. Before creating your Web site, think about who your most likely customers are, what types of ads appeal to them, and what Web browsers they are likely to own. These issues will help you decide what features your site must have and what features waste your marketing dollars.

Design your site to look like your other marketing materials, with the same colors, logos, and backgrounds that appeal to your target market. Otherwise, your Internet customers will think they are at the wrong site. Lone Star Technical displays the Texas flag on both its site and its other marketing collateral.

A Web site is more like a store than an advertisement: you must work to get customers to visit. Put the address on your business cards and letterhead and in your telephone directory ads and brochures. Mike even posted his on the U.S. Small Business Administration's Web site.

Finally, every the business owner must devote time each week to answering e-mail from the Web site and participating in user groups to attract more attention to the site.

# *101.* THE WRITE WAY

Writing articles for targeted publications can be more effective marketing than paid advertising.

■ ■ ■

**R**obert Joyce had been a business consultant and management trainer for years when a major corporation offered him a job that Robert figured would carry him until retirement. The recession of the early 1990s killed that plan when Robert was laid off. Instead of going back to his old consulting routine, however, Robert wanted a new challenge. He was intrigued by the idea of helping older people write and publish their personal and family histories as keepsakes for their children; therefore, in 1993, he established Hawthorne House in his Santa Ana, California, home to do just that.

"I knew how to run a business, but I had no idea how to reach my customers," Robert says. "It was just gut instinct that people would be interested in this service."

Robert took $10,000 from his 401(k) plan to develop name identity for his company. He bought display advertising in five different magazines targeted at older Americans. Small two-inch-by-two-inch ads cost $200 a month, so it didn't take long to spend the $10,000.

"Although I got a couple of jobs, it wasn't cost effective," Robert says. "An even bigger mistake was not discontinuing the ads earlier than I did. Any money I made I poured back into more ads."

Finally, Robert discovered that the writing skill he used to create his product was also a valuable marketing device.

First, he wrote a sample family history, which he showed to prospective customers. Then he found another way to leverage his writing.

"I began to write articles for some of the seniors magazines, and they would usually list my company name, phone number, and address with the articles," Robert says. "Also, a couple of magazines did short write-ups on me because my business was so unusual."

Both types of articles gave credibility to both Robert and Hawthorne House, he says. He received more inquiries and more jobs from these articles than his display ads ever brought.

Forget what you've heard about the demise of the written word. More than 20,000 magazines are published in the United States alone, and between 800 and 1,000 new ones start each year. Ninety-five percent of them target specialized markets. If you or one of your employees can write articles of interest to your target customer, chances are the magazines that target that same audience will consider publishing them. They may even pay you, but at least they should include your name, your company, and how to reach you.

Robert determined which publications were most likely to be read by his most probable buyer. Then he studied those publications to find out how his information or articles might fit in. Some publications invite reader participation. Many have new product listings, tips of the month, or industry notes. Often one paragraph elicits greater reader response than a long article.

Business owners who want to write for marketing benefits must keep in mind that the information or articles probably won't be printed if they're nothing more than free ads. The writing that gets published shares new information, tells a dramatic tale, or offers useful tips. Robert can write about how to trace genealogies, what makes an anecdote interesting, or ten items in your attic your kids will wonder about after you're gone.

Robert also has found ways to expand the benefit he reaps from responses to his articles.

"Every single person who called went on my master mailing list," Robert says. "I mail regularly to 500 people. If they don't want their family histories written now, they might change their minds later. Or they might pass on my information to someone they know."

After three years in business, Robert added his own newsletter to his marketing writing. He mails it out three times a year.

"It's an excellent, low-cost way to stay in touch with people who have contacted me," Robert says. "One person might not be interested, but will have a sister-in-law who is. I never know when my newsletter is going to be passed on."

**TIPS...**

**86.** Find the experts who will help educate consumers to a new product.

**87.** Take time and care to plan your marketing strategy and budget to make most effective use of your time and money.

**88.** Invest in marketing, just as you would invest in a good business suit, professional letterhead, and business cards.

**89.** Focus your attention and resources on a few high-potential skill areas.

**90.** Have enough customers that the loss of one won't bankrupt your company.

**91.** Highly skilled technicians must practice selling their sizzle in well-crafted presentations.

**92.** Never miss an opportunity to ask potential customers for ideas that will improve your business.

**93.** Never underestimate the schmooze factor in building your business.

**94.** Some of the least expensive types of marketing are most effective in building a new business.

**95.** If you have endless fistfuls of money to throw at finding customers, marketing is a numbers game. Otherwise, spend money on the people most likely to buy from you.

**96.** People do business with people they know. Just make sure you're getting to know the people you can do business with.

**97.** Albert Einstein said of science that if you can't explain it simply, you don't understand it well enough. The same is true in business.

**98.** Make sure your commercial lease and local ordinances allow your business to post an adequate sign to tell people who and where you are.

**99.** Public speaking should benefit both your business and your audience. Entertain and inform; don't bore and brag.

**100.** Don't throw a lot of money into Internet advertising until you understand how the Internet works. However, don't delay finding out; this is one fast-moving medium.

**101.** Share your knowledge in written articles and newsletters for another win-win way to market your company.

# APPENDIX

## INTERNET RESOURCE GUIDE

### GOVERNMENT

**Census Bureau**
www.census.gov
Plenty of economic and demographic reports. Click on news, then census briefs, to reach full reports for your area.

**European patents**
www.epo.co.at/epo
Information about the European Patent Office, created in 1973 to establish a uniform patent system in Europe.

**Federal Government**
www.business.gov
Information for all federal sites helpful to businesses in one place.

**Federal Reserve Board**
www.bog.frb.fed.us
*National Survey of Small Business Finances, Bank Lending Practices,* other studies by the Federal Reserve.

**Federal Small Business Innovation and Research**
www.inknowvation.com
Information about the SBIR grant program, which helps small companies develop technological innovation, economic impact, and business achievement.

**Government Contracting**
www.govcon.com
Information for government contractors, including *Commerce Business Daily,* lists of government contracting officials, articles, discussion groups.

## Government Printing Office
www.access.gpo.gov
Wide array of reports and studies and other publications available from federal agencies.

## National Technology Transfer Center
www.nttc.edu
Information about the center, which provides technical assistance and grant opportunities, information about assistance from the Department of Defense, NASA, and small-business development centers, inventors' resources, technical briefs.

## 1996 White House Conference on Small Business
www.whcsb.org:81
Legislative issues of importance to small business, delegates' names, recommendations from this gathering of small-business owners.
www.whcsb.com
Another site generated out of the conference, delegates' names, small-business resources, business advertising.

## Securities and Exchange Commission
www.sec.gov
Online access to filings that public companies must make, small-business information, current SEC rulemaking.

## Service Corps of Retired Executives
www.score.org
Useful information from SCORE's volunteer counselors plus success stories.

## U.S. House of Representatives Committee on Small Business
www.house.gov/smbiz
Legislation, members, small-business facts, news releases, monthly bulletins.

## U.S. Patent and Trademark Office
www.USPTO.gov
Wealth of information about how to search for existing patents and apply for new patents, as well as filing fees.

## U.S. Senate Small Business Committee
www.senate.gov/~sbc/
Legislation affecting small businesses, committee publications, news releases, members, hearing schedule.

**U.S. Small Business Administration**
www.sba.gov
Information on starting, financing, and running a small business, many programs for small businesses, links to other useful government sites.

# COMPANIES

**American Express**
www.americanexpress.com/smallbusiness/
Information-rich site for small business owners.

**Bookkeeping, Income Tax & Small Business Help Online**
www.geocities.com/WallStreet/2924/list1.htm
Informative articles on business planning, incorporation, start-up costs, and more, from Grable Tax Services.

**Claris Corp.**
www.claris.com/smallbiz
Expert advice on everything from online marketing to building customer relations to financial issues.

**Deloitte & Touche LLP**
www.datonline.com/ba/ba.htm
Information in SIMPLE retirement plans, effects of new tax laws on small business, global expansion for small firms.

**Khera Communications, Inc.**
www.morebusiness.com
Sample business agreements, free time-saving templates, expert advice.

**LEXIS-NEXIS**
www.lexis-nexis.com/bizlog4sb
Answers to starting and managing a small business, articles on ethics for businesses and on other topics, links to other business sites.

**Microsoft Corp.**
www.microsoft.com/smallbiz
Buyer's guides, work information, customer success stories, expert advice on small-business management.

**Small Business Advisor**
www.isquare.com
Advice for small-business professionals, created by Information International consulting firm.

**Visa**
www.visa.com/cgi-bin/vee/fb/smlbiz/main.html
Tips, monthly survey results, daily news tips for businesses.

# ASSOCIATIONS

**American Association of Home-Based Businesses**
www.aahbb.org
Articles written by members, including "Choosing a Lawyer," "Choosing an Accountant," and "Professional Image."

**American Home Business Association**
www.homebusiness.com
Information on starting, financing, and running a business from home.

**American Payroll Association**
www.americanpayroll.org/new
Information about new standard mileage rate, proposals to simplify verification of workers' immigration statuses, and more.

**Home Office Association of America**
www.hoaa.com
Information for starting and running a business from home.

**National Association for the Self-Employed**
www.nase.org
Legislative updates, articles from *Self-Employed America* magazine, reference section.

**National Federation of Independent Business**
www.nfibonline.com
Reports on legislative action on bills that affect small businesses, other news from this Washington, D.C.–based lobbying group.

**National Foundation of Women Business Owners**
www.nfwbo.org
Data on women business owners and studies of women entrepreneurs' work habits, based on research done by the foundation for the National Association of Women Business Owners.

**National Minority Business Council, Inc.**
www.nmbc.org
Business referrals, international trade information, publications.

**SOHO America**
www.soho.org
Reference tools, tips, news, from SOHO (small office home office).

# FRANCHISING

**American Association of Franchisees & Dealers**
www.aafd.org
Tips, programs, publications, for franchisees.

*Business Opportunities Handbook*
www.ezines.com
Listing of 2,500 companies selling franchises, vending machines, mail-order businesses, and distributorships.

*Franchise Annual*
www.vaxxine.com/franchise
Online version of publication of thousands of franchising opportunities, tips for investigating a franchise, Info Franchise Newsletter, litigation issues.

**International Franchise Association**
www.franchise.org
Resources, government issues, other information, for franchisers, franchisees, and people considering either role.

# PUBLICATIONS

### American Demographics
www.marketingtools.com
Back issues of *Marketing Tools* magazine, articles on and sources of business demographics, other sources useful in market research.

### *Business@Home* magazine
www.gohome.com
Online version of print magazine, with information for home-based business owners and telecommuters.

### Dearborn Publishing
www.dearborn.com
Small-business books.

### *Entrepreneur* magazine
www.entrepreneurmag.com
Online versions of *Entrepreneur, Business Start-ups, Entrepreneur Home Office,* and *Entrepreneur International* magazines.

### *Hispanic Business* magazine
http://hispanicbusiness.com
Information, articles, for Hispanic business owners.

### *Home Office Computing*
www.smalloffice.com
Office equipment, tools, tips, trade information.

### *Inc.* magazine
www.inc.com
Past articles from *Inc.*, bulletin boards, interactive worksheets, help creating a Web site.

### Nolo Press
www.nolopress.com
Do-it-yourself legal books, hundreds of tips and articles for small-business owners.

# FINANCING

### America's Business Funding Directory
www.businessfinanc.com
Sources, resources, information, for entrepreneurs looking for financing.

### Venture Capital Database
www.datamerge
Free venture capital database, information on small corporate offering registration, matching service, from financing software publisher DataMerge.

### Venture Capital Marketplace
www.v-capital.com.au
Forum for private companies trying to raise capital and for individual and corporate investors seeking investment opportunities in companies that meet certain criteria.

### Out of Your Mind and into the Marketplace
www.pubisness-plan.com
What information to include in a business plan; real-life examples of business plans from author Linda Pinson.

# DIRECT MARKETING

### Direct Marketing Association
www.the-dma.org
Direct mail guidelines, such as ethical business practices, fact sheets, and various direct marketing events.

### Direct Marketing Dynamics
www.dmsource.com
Rich with information about direct marketing; list of recommended direct marketing resources.

### Direct Marketing Response
www.nlci.com/response
Packed with information on how to cut direct mail costs, improve response rates, and more, from direct mail copy designer Ron Ferguson.

# INTERNATIONAL TRADE

### Export Information
www.tradecompas.com
Database of trade information for 190 countries and 600 different commodities to help visitors identify largest markets for their products, up-to-date data, such as foreign exchange rates.

### International Trade Associations
www.webhead.comFITA/home.html
Directory of business groups, trade clubs, and associations involved in import and export, articles on international trade topics.

# MISCELLANEOUS

### All Business Network
www.all-biz.com
News, job bank, online databases, business services, articles on a wide range of business ownership topics.

### Entrepreneurial Education
www.celcee.edu
Clearinghouse of entrepreneurial education from kindergarten through graduate school, from the Ewing Marion Kauffman Foundation.

### Find an Area Code
www.cse.ucsd.edu/users/bsy/area.html
Current area codes and former codes from which the new ones split.

### Idea Café
www.ideacafe.com
Information and resources for small-business professionals, especially those just starting out.

### Shipping Rates
www.smartship.com
Information to help business shippers compare current prices of Federal Express, United Parcel, and other shipping firms, from software company Vitran, Inc.

**Small Business Net**

www.lowe.org/smbiznet

More than 4,000 documents from government agencies, small-business consultants, and entrepreneurial books, from the Edward Lowe Foundation.

**Smart Business Supersite**

www.smartbiz.com

How-to resources, news briefs, listing of trade shows.

# Web Sites of Businesses in This Book

1. Wendy's International, *www.wendys.com*
3. National Microcomp Services, *www.nmservice.com*
7. Box Connection, *www.boxconnection.com*
9. Financial Education Publishers, Inc./Oyster Communications, *www.oystercommunications.com*
10. Association of Business Support Services, Inc., *www.abssi.org*
11. Preferred Industrial Services, Inc., *www.preferredinc.com*
12. Carolina PetSpace, *www.citysearch.com/rdu/petspace*
13. The Chocolate Tree, *www.islc.net/business/choctree/*
14. EagleRider Motorcycle Rental USA, *www.eaglerider.com*
15. AGSCO, *www.agsco.com*
16. Laurey's Catering, *www.laureysyum.com*
18. People Dynamics, *www.thedynamicsgroup.com*
19. 1-888-Inn-Seek, *www.innseekers.com*
20. Blackburn Manufacturing, *www.blackburnflag.com*
29. Omni Tech, *www.otcwi.com*
30. Mills/James Productions, *www.millsjames.com*
31. Taquan Air Service, Inc., *www.alaskaone.com/TaquanAir/*
32. Newsletter Resources, *www.newsletterinfo.com*
33. W. Gozdz Enterprises, Inc., *www.wgozdz.com*
34. Kott Koatings, Inc., *www.kottkoatings.com*
35. Ohm Corporation, *www.ohmcorp.com*
36. Lillian Vernon Corp., *www.lillianvernon.com*
41. Hsu's Ginseng Enterprises, Inc., *www.hsuginseng.com*
42. Coffee Beanery (franchising company), *www.coffeebeanery.com*
43. Mommy Times, *www.mommytimes.com*
45. Fitness International, *www.fitnessinternational.com*
47. Deluxe Color Printers, *www.deluxecolor.com*
48. Royce Instrument Corp., *www.royceinst.com*
49. Special Order Systems, *www.team-sos.com*

53. CKE, Inc., *www.carlsjr.com*
56. JMG Security Systems, *www.securityresource.com*
58. Construction Notebook News, *www.constructionnotebook.com*
59. Independent Small Business Employers of America, Inc.,
    *www.employerhelp.org*
60. Rowena's, Inc., *www.pilotonline.com/rowenas*
62. Downtime, Inc., *www.downtime.com*
63. Wright-K Technology, Inc., *www.wright-k.com*
65. Heart Enterprises, *www.galaxymall.com/product/lampshade*
66. Haas Outdoors, Inc., *www.mossyoak.com*
67. Rose Wing Consulting and Grant Writing,
    *www.galaxymall.com/finance/rosewing*
69. Austin Food Tech, *www.austinfoodtech.com*
71. Zick Communications, Inc., *www.zick.com*
73. Sorensen Moving & Storage, *www.sorensen-allied.com*
74. Telephone Doctor, *www.teldoc.com*
75. Lontos Sales & Motivation, *www.PamLontos.com*
76. JB Chemical Co., *www.jbchem.com*
78. RVI II, *www.rvi2.com*
79. Focus Publications, *www.focusoc.com*
80. Badmoon Books, *www.horrorcollector.com/badmoon.htm*
83. Diana's California Cookies, *www.californiacookies.com*
85. Rosco Manufacturing, *www.sdibi.northern.edu/Rosco/Ros_home.htm*
86. Optiva Corp., *www.optiva.com*
88. PDQ Personnel Services, *www.pdqcareers.com*
89. Information Management Resources, Inc., *www.imri.com*
91. InterScience, Inc., *www.intersci.com*
92. Venture Outdoors, *www.webpack.net/~venout*
93. Pacifica Services, Inc., *www.pacifica-services-inc.com*
94. Confidante Keys, *www.cruznet.net/~ckeys*
96. Escoe/Bliss Communications, *http://home.earthlink.net/~escoebliss*
100. Dentrep 2000, *www.ultrasonicrepair.com*
101. Hawthorne House, *www.bookzone.com/hawthorne*

Jan Norman, *www.smallbusinessresources.com*

# INDEX